Best Quick Fixes

This book is printed on acid-free paper.

Published by John Wiley & Sons, Inc., Hoboken, New Jersey

For general information on our other products and services or for technical support, please contact our Customer Care Department within the United States at (800) 762–2974, outside the United States at (317) 572–3993 or fax (317) 572–4002.

Wiley also publishes its books in a variety of electronic formats. Some content that appears in print may not be available in electronic books. For more information about Wiley products, visit our web site at www.wiley.com.

Library of Congress Cataloging-in-Publication Data:

Best quick fixes / by ACP Books.
      p. cm.
   Includes index.
   ISBN 978-0-470-44055-1 (pbk.)
   1. Cookery. I. ACP Books. II. ACP Magazines Ltd.
   TX714.B455 2009
   641.5'55—dc22

Printed in the United States of America

10 9 8 7 6 5 4 3 2 1

Designed for the busy home cook, *Best Quick Fixes* provides a wide range of tempting recipes for every night of the week. Fresh, simple ingredients can create satisfying and healthy meals in a flash. Every recipe in this collection can be on the table in around half an hour.

Contents

light meals   6

pasta   64

poultry   116

seafood   182

beef & veal   228

pork   300

lamb   338

index   369

Light Meals

Sometimes a savory snack or hearty salad is just what you crave. These are perfect dishes for lunch or a midweek dinner — tasty and satisfying.

shrimp fritters with avocado salsa

preparation time 20 minutes **cooking time** 10 minutes **serves** 4

1 pound cooked large shrimp

3 tablespoons olive oil

1 medium onion, chopped coarsely

1 clove garlic, crushed

2 teaspoons hot paprika

½ teaspoon ground cumin

¼ teaspoon ground white pepper

¼ teaspoon cayenne pepper

1 ½ cups self-rising flour

2 eggs

1 ½ cups milk

1 ½ tablespoons coarsely chopped
  fresh chives

2 medium avocados (about 1 pound),
  chopped coarsely

2 medium tomatoes, chopped coarsely

1 green onion, sliced thinly

3 tablespoons fresh lime juice

1 Peel and devein shrimp; chop shrimp coarsely.

2 Heat half of the oil in large non-stick skillet; cook onion, garlic and spices, stirring, until onion softens.

3 Place flour in large bowl; stir in combined eggs and milk, stir until smooth. Stir in chives, onion mixture and shrimp.

4 Heat remaining oil in same cleaned skillet; cook ¼-cups of shrimp mixture, in batches, until browned on both sides.

5 Combine remaining ingredients in medium bowl. Serve fritters with avocado salsa.

Tip Fritter batter can be prepared 4 hours ahead; cover, refrigerate.

NUTRITIONAL INFO PER SERVING 37g total fat (9g saturated fat); 49g carbohydrate; 27g protein; 5g fiber; 643 calories

chicken Caesar salad

preparation time 5 minutes   **cooking time** 20 minutes   **serves** 4

4 slices white bread

3 tablespoons olive oil

7 thick slices bacon (10 ounces),
    sliced thinly

3 cups (1 pound) coarsely chopped
    rotisserie chicken

1 large head Romaine lettuce, chopped

6 green onions, sliced thinly

1 cup shaved parmesan cheese

Caesar dressing

¾ cup mayonnaise

1 ½ tablespoons fresh lemon juice

4 drained anchovy fillets, chopped finely

3 teaspoons Dijon mustard

1 ½ tablespoons water

1 Preheat oven to 350°F.

2 Make Caesar dressing.

3 Remove crusts from bread; discard crusts, cut bread into ¾-inch squares; toss with oil in medium bowl. Place bread, in single layer, on baking sheet; toast in oven, 10 minutes.

4 Cook bacon in small skillet, stirring, until browned. Drain on paper towels.

5 Combine half of the chicken, half of the bacon, half of the croutons and half of the dressing in large bowl with lettuce, half of the onions and half of the cheese; toss gently to combine.

6 Divide salad among serving plates. Top with remaining chicken, bacon, croutons, onions and cheese; drizzle with remaining dressing.

Caesar dressing Blend or process ingredients until mixture is smooth.

Tip You'll need to purchase a large rotisserie chicken weighing 2 pounds to get 3 cups of chopped chicken.

NUTRITIONAL INFO PER SERVING 50g total fat (12g saturated fat); 36g carbohydrate; 53g protein; 6g fiber; 811 calories

poached eggs with sage brown butter and asparagus

preparation time 10 minutes **cooking time** 10 minutes **serves** 4

6 tablespoons butter

12 fresh sage leaves

4 eggs

7 ounces asparagus, trimmed

4 English muffins

1 ½ ounces shaved parmesan cheese

1 Melt butter in small pot; cook sage, stirring, about 3 minutes or until butter changes color to deep brown. Remove from heat; cover to keep warm.

2 Half-fill a shallow skillet with water; bring to a boil. One at a time, break eggs into cup, then slide into pan. When all eggs are in skillet, allow water to return to a boil. Cover skillet, turn off heat; let stand about 4 minutes or until a light film of egg white sets over yolks. One at a time, remove eggs, using spatula, and place on paper towel-lined saucer to blot up poaching liquid.

3 Boil, steam or microwave asparagus until tender. Drain; cover to keep warm. Split muffins; toast.

4 Place bottom halves of muffins on serving plates; top each with equal amounts of asparagus, an egg, 1 ½ tablespoons of sage butter, and cheese. Serve with remaining muffin halves.

Tip When poaching the eggs, don't lift the lid during poaching as the steam helps set the eggs.

NUTRITIONAL INFO PER SERVING 26g total fat (15g saturated fat); 24g carbohydrate; 18g protein; 2g fiber; 403 calories

spinach, feta and red pepper pizza

preparation time 10 minutes **cooking time** 10 minutes **serves** 4

4 large rounds pita bread

⅔ cup pasta sauce

2 cups coarsely grated mozzarella cheese

2 ½ cups baby spinach

1 medium red bell pepper, sliced thinly

3 ½ ounces feta cheese, crumbled

1 Preheat oven to 475°F.

2 Place two rounds of pita on each of two baking sheets; spread each piece with sauce then sprinkle half of the mozzarella over all four pieces. Top with spinach, bell pepper and feta; sprinkle with remaining mozzarella.

3 Bake pizza, uncovered, about 10 minutes or until cheese melts and pizza crusts are crisp.

NUTRITIONAL INFO PER SERVING 21g total fat (12g saturated fat); 63g carbohydrate; 32g protein; 5g fiber; 579 calories

panzanella salad

preparation time 15 minutes **cooking time** 10 minutes **serves** 4

½ long loaf ciabatta or other crusty
   Italian bread (8 ounces)
1 clove garlic, crushed
¼ cup olive oil
1 pound cherry tomatoes, halved
1 cucumber, seeded, sliced thinly
1 medium avocado, chopped coarsely
¼ cup drained capers, rinsed
1 large yellow bell pepper,
   chopped coarsely
two 14 ½-ounce cans cannellini or
   Great Northern beans, rinsed, drained
½ cup coarsely chopped fresh basil

Tomato vinaigrette
½ cup tomato juice
¼ cup red wine vinegar
⅓ cup olive oil

1 Preheat oven to 400°F.
2 Cut bread into 1-inch cubes. Combine bread in large bowl with combined garlic and oil; toss to coat bread in oil mixture. Place bread, in single layer, on baking sheet; bake about 10 minutes or until browned lightly.
3 Make tomato vinaigrette.
4 Place bread in same large bowl with remaining ingredients and vinaigrette; toss gently to combine.
Tomato vinaigrette Whisk together all ingredients.

NUTRITIONAL INFO PER SERVING 45g total fat (7g saturated fat); 58g carbohydrate; 16g protein; 13g fiber; 706 calories

beef salad with fennel and balsamic vinaigrette

preparation time 15 minutes (plus standing time) **cooking time** 15 minutes **serves** 4

3 ½ ounces bean thread noodles

4 rib-eye steaks (1 ¾ pounds)

2 medium fennel bulbs (1 ¼ pounds),
   sliced thinly

1 medium red onion, sliced thinly

5 cups baby arugula

1 ¼ cups shaved parmesan cheese

Balsamic vinaigrette

¼ cup fresh lemon juice

2 cloves garlic, crushed

¼ cup olive oil

3 tablespoons balsamic vinegar

1 ½ tablespoons coarsely chopped
   fresh thyme

1 Place noodles in medium heatproof bowl; cover with boiling water, let stand until just tender, drain.

2 Make balsamic vinaigrette.

3 Cook steaks on heated oiled grill or grill pan until browned on both sides and cooked as desired. Cover; let stand 5 minutes.

4 Cut noodles into 2-inch lengths; place in large bowl with fennel, onion and arugula. Slice steak thinly, add to noodles with balsamic vinaigrette; toss gently to combine. Serve salad topped with cheese.

Balsamic vinaigrette Whisk together all ingredients.

NUTRITIONAL INFO PER SERVING 35g total fat (12g saturated fat); 23g carbohydrate; 56g protein; 4g fiber; 632 calories

grilled vegetable and ricotta stack

preparation time 20 minutes **cooking time** 30 minutes **serves** 4

2 baby eggplants, sliced thickly lengthwise

1 medium green bell pepper,
   sliced thickly lengthwise

1 medium red bell pepper,
   sliced thickly lengthwise

2 large zucchini, sliced thickly lengthwise

four 6-ounce portabella mushrooms,
   stems removed

2 cups ricotta cheese

2 cloves garlic, crushed

½ cup coarsely chopped fresh basil

3 tablespoons finely chopped fresh chives

1 ½ tablespoons coarsely chopped
   fresh oregano

1 ½ tablespoons finely grated lemon peel

3 tablespoons toasted pine nuts

Sun-dried tomato pesto

¼ cup drained sun-dried tomatoes, halved

½ cup firmly packed fresh basil

3 tablespoons balsamic vinegar

3 tablespoons water

1 Cook eggplants, bell peppers, zucchini and mushrooms, in batches, on heated oiled grill or grill pan until tender.

2 Combine cheese, garlic, herbs and lemon peel in medium bowl.

3 Make sun-dried tomato pesto.

4 Divide mushrooms, stem-side up, among serving plates; layer with cheese mixture, slices of eggplant, zucchini and bell pepper. Drizzle with pesto; sprinkle with nuts.

Sun-dried tomato pesto Blend or process tomato and basil until mixture forms a paste. With motor running, gradually add combined vinegar and water in thin, steady stream until pesto is smooth.

NUTRITIONAL INFO PER SERVING 18g total fat (8g saturated fat); 11g carbohydrate; 21g protein; 10g fiber; 288 calories

steak salad with blue cheese dressing

preparation time 10 minutes (plus standing time) **cooking time** 20 minutes **serves** 4

1 pound new potatoes, quartered

1 ½ tablespoons olive oil

4 filet mignon steaks (1 pound)

10 ounces green beans, halved crosswise

7 ounces grape tomatoes, halved

3 ½ cups baby arugula

Blue cheese dressing

¼ cup olive oil

2 cloves garlic, crushed

¼ cup orange juice

2 ounces blue cheese, crumbled

1 Preheat oven to 475°F.

2 Place potatoes, in single layer, in large shallow baking dish; drizzle with oil. Roast, uncovered, about 20 minutes or until lightly browned and tender.

3 Make blue cheese dressing.

4 Cook steaks on heated oiled grill or grill pan until browned on both sides and cooked as desired. Cover; let stand 5 minutes.

5 Boil, steam or microwave beans until just tender; drain.

6 Slice steak thinly. Combine steak, beans and potatoes in large bowl with tomatoes and arugula, drizzle with blue cheese dressing; toss gently to combine.

Blue cheese dressing Whisk together all ingredients.

NUTRITIONAL INFO PER SERVING 31g total fat (9g saturated fat); 21g carbohydrate; 35g protein; 6g fiber; 515 calories

Thai beef salad

preparation time 25 minutes (plus refrigeration time) **cooking time** 10 minutes **serves** 4

One of everyone's favorites at the local Thai restaurant, our version of "yum nuah" is so easy to prepare and so delicious, you'll be making it at home from now on.

¼ cup fish sauce

¼ cup fresh lime juice

1 pound sirloin steak

3 small cucumbers, seeded, sliced thinly

4 Thai chilies or 2 jalapeño peppers, sliced thinly

4 green onions, sliced thinly

8 ounces cherry tomatoes, halved

¼ cup firmly packed fresh mint

½ cup firmly packed fresh cilantro

½ cup firmly packed fresh basil

1 ½ tablespoons brown sugar

2 teaspoons soy sauce

1 clove garlic, crushed

1 Combine 3 tablespoons of the fish sauce and 1 ½ tablespoons of the lime juice in medium bowl, add beef; toss beef to coat in marinade. Cover; refrigerate until ready to use.

2 Drain beef; discard marinade. Cook beef on heated oiled grill or grill pan until cooked as desired. Cover, beef, let stand 5 minutes; slice beef thinly.

3 Combine cucumber, chilies, onions, tomatoes and herbs in bowl.

4 Whisk together sugar, soy sauce, garlic, remaining fish sauce and lime juice. Add beef and dressing to salad; toss gently to combine.

Tip If possible, marinate meat the night before serving so the flavors can penetrate the beef.

NUTRITIONAL INFO PER SERVING 9g total fat (4g saturated fat); 8g carbohydrate; 31g protein; 3g fiber; 986 calories

Greek pasta salad

preparation time 15 minutes **cooking time** 15 minutes **serves** 6

1 ¼ pounds boneless lamb steaks

1 ½ tablespoons olive oil

1 ½ tablespoons finely chopped
   fresh oregano

1 pound rigatoni pasta

1 medium red onion, cut into thin wedges

1 pound cherry tomatoes, halved

2 small cucumbers, chopped coarsely

1 large green bell pepper,
   chopped coarsely

1 ⅔ cups seeded Kalamata olives

7 ounces feta cheese, crumbled

Lemon oregano dressing

½ cup olive oil

½ cup fresh lemon juice

1 ½ tablespoons finely chopped
   fresh oregano

1 Combine lamb, oil and one third of the oregano in large bowl. Cook lamb, in batches, in oiled nonstick skillet until browned and cooked as desired. Cover lamb; let stand 5 minutes, slice thinly.

2 Cook pasta in large pot of boiling salted water, uncovered, until just tender; drain. Rinse under cold water; drain.

3 Make lemon oregano dressing.

4 Place lamb and pasta in large bowl with onion, tomatoes, cucumbers, bell pepper, olives and dressing; toss gently to combine. Top with cheese; sprinkle with remaining oregano.

Lemon oregano dressing Whisk together all ingredients.

NUTRITIONAL INFO PER SERVING 40g total fat (12g saturated fat); 72g carbohydrate; 38g protein; 7g fiber; 803 calories

Chinese barbecued duck salad

preparation time 30 minutes **cooking time** 5 minutes **serves** 4

If you can't find Chinese barbecued duck, try this salad with a rotisserie roasted chicken.

1 Chinese barbecued duck
7 ounces dried rice stick noodles
¾ cup loosely packed fresh cilantro
¾ cup loosely packed fresh mint
2 cucumbers, seeded, sliced thinly
½ cup roasted cashews

Chili lime dressing
1-2 jalapeño peppers, seeded,
   chopped finely
1 stalk fresh lemongrass, chopped finely
1 clove garlic, crushed
1 teaspoon coarsely grated lime peel
¼ cup fresh lime juice
3 tablespoons peanut oil
1½ tablespoons brown sugar
1½ tablespoons fish sauce
2 teaspoons sesame oil

1 Discard skin and bones from duck; chop meat coarsely.
2 Place noodles in medium heatproof bowl, cover with boiling water, let stand until just tender; drain. Rinse under cold water; drain.
3 Make chili lime dressing.
4 Combine duck and noodles in large bowl with herbs and cucumber, drizzle with dressing; toss gently to combine. Top with nuts before serving.
Chili lime dressing Whisk together all ingredients.

NUTRITIONAL INFO PER SERVING 59g total fat (15g saturated fat); 41g carbohydrate; 36g protein; 4g fiber; 834 calories

endive salad with shrimp, pink grapefruit and lime aïoli

preparation time 30 minutes **serves** 4

3 pink grapefruit (about 2 pounds)

2 pounds cooked large shrimp

12 ounces curly endive, torn

¼ cup coarsely chopped chives

2 celery stalks, sliced thinly

1 small red onion, sliced thinly

Lime aïoli

2 egg yolks

2 teaspoons Dijon mustard

½ teaspoon finely grated lime peel

3 tablespoons fresh lime juice

2 cloves garlic, quartered

¾ cup light olive oil

1 ½ tablespoons hot water

1 Make lime aïoli.

2 Peel grapefruit; separate the segments. Peel and devein shrimp, leaving tails intact.

3 Combine grapefruit and shrimp in large serving bowl with remaining ingredients. Serve with lime aïoli.

Lime aïoli Blend or process egg yolks, mustard, lime peel, lime juice and garlic until combined. With motor running, gradually add oil, blending until aïoli thickens. With motor running, add enough of the water (if any) to achieve desired consistency.

Tip Lime aïoli can be prepared a day ahead; keep covered in the refrigerator.

NUTRITIONAL INFO PER SERVING 45g total fat (7g saturated fat); 10g carbohydrate; 31g protein; 4g fiber; 575 calories

Asian chicken salad

preparation time 20 minutes **cooking time** 10 minutes **serves** 4

2 cups water

2 cups chicken stock

4 boneless, skinless chicken breasts
   (1 ½ pounds)

1 small red bell pepper, sliced thinly

4 radishes, sliced thinly

¼ small Chinese cabbage,
   shredded coarsely

3 green onions, sliced thinly

1 cup bean sprouts

½ cup loosely packed fresh cilantro

½ cup roasted salted peanuts

Chili lime dressing

⅓ cup fresh lime juice

¼ cup brown sugar

2 fresh small red serrano or Thai chilies,
   chopped finely

1 clove garlic, crushed

1 ½ tablespoons fish sauce

¼ cup peanut oil

1 Bring the water and stock to a boil in large skillet. Add chicken, reduce heat; simmer, covered, about 10 minutes or until cooked through. Remove from heat; cool chicken in liquid 10 minutes. Slice chicken thinly.

2 Make chili lime dressing.

3 Place remaining ingredients and half of the dressing in large bowl; toss gently to combine.

4 Divide salad among plates; top with chicken, drizzle with remaining dressing.

Chili lime dressing Combine lime juice, sugar, chilies and garlic in small pot. Stir over low heat until sugar dissolves; cool 10 minutes. Whisk in fish sauce and oil.

NUTRITIONAL INFO PER SERVING 27g total fat (4g saturated fat); 22g carbohydrate; 47g protein; 4g fiber; 516 calories

pork, lime and peanut salad

preparation time 25 minutes (plus refrigeration time) **cooking time** 15 minutes **serves** 4

¼ cup fresh lime juice

1 ½-inch piece fresh ginger, grated

1 ¾ pounds pork loin chops, sliced thinly

1 pound broccoli rabe or Swiss chard, chopped coarsely

3 tablespoons water

3 large carrots, cut into matchsticks

½ cup firmly packed fresh basil

1 cup firmly packed fresh cilantro

4 green onions, sliced thinly

¼ cup coarsely chopped roasted peanuts

Sweet chili dressing

1 ½ tablespoons fish sauce

1 ½ tablespoons sweet Thai chili sauce

3 tablespoons fresh lime juice

1 fresh small red serrano or Thai chili, chopped finely (optional)

1 Combine lime juice and ginger in large bowl, add pork; toss pork to coat in marinade. Cover; refrigerate 3 hours or overnight.

2 Make sweet chili dressing.

3 Stir-fry pork, in batches, in heated lightly oiled wok or skillet until cooked as desired. Cover to keep warm. Stir-fry broccoli rabe with the water in same pan until just wilted.

4 Place pork, broccoli rabe and dressing in large bowl with carrots, herbs and onions; toss gently to combine. Sprinkle with nuts.

Sweet chili dressing Whisk together all ingredients.

NUTRITIONAL INFO PER SERVING 10g total fat (2g saturated fat); 7g carbohydrate; 49g protein; 5g fiber; 321 calories

grilled octopus salad

preparation time 15 minutes **cooking time** 5 minutes **serves** 4

⅓ cup fresh orange juice

1 ½ tablespoons fresh lemon juice

⅔ cup olive oil

1 clove garlic, crushed

1 ¼ pounds cleaned baby octopus

1 cup pitted Kalamata olives

5 small cucumbers (about 1 ¼ pounds),
   seeded, chopped coarsely

7 ounces grape tomatoes, halved

⅓ cup coarsely chopped fresh
   flat-leaf parsley

1 Whisk together orange juice, lemon juice, oil and garlic.

2 Cook octopus, in batches, on heated oiled grill or grill pan until browned lightly and cooked as desired. Do not overcook.

3 Toss octopus and dressing in medium bowl, add olives, cucumber, tomato and parsley; toss gently to combine.

NUTRITIONAL INFO PER SERVING 38g total fat (5g saturated fat); 14g carbohydrate; 26g protein; 3g fiber; 504 calories

pan-fried tofu with cabbage salad

preparation time 20 minutes **cooking time** 15 minutes **serves** 4

You'll need about half a Chinese cabbage for this recipe.

three 10 ½-ounce pieces firm silken tofu

1 ½ tablespoons finely chopped
   fresh lemongrass

2 fresh small red serrano or Thai chilies,
   sliced thinly (optional)

1 medium red onion, sliced thinly

1 cup bean sprouts

4 cups finely shredded Chinese cabbage

¾ cup firmly packed fresh cilantro

Sweet and sour dressing

⅓ cup fresh lime juice

2 teaspoons brown sugar

3 tablespoons soy sauce

1 Pat tofu all over with paper towels. Slice each tofu piece vertically into four slices. Place tofu slices, in single layer, on paper towel-lined baking sheet; cover tofu with more paper towels, let stand at least 10 minutes.

2 Make sweet and sour dressing.

3 Cook tofu, in batches, in large heated lightly oiled skillet until browned on both sides.

4 Place remaining ingredients in large bowl; toss gently to combine.

5 Divide salad among serving plates; top with tofu, drizzle with dressing.

Sweet and sour dressing Whisk together all ingredients until sugar disolves.

NUTRITIONAL INFO PER SERVING 16g total fat (2g saturated fat); 8g carbohydrate; 30g protein; 7g fiber; 295 calories

shrimp and avocado salad with ginger dressing

preparation time 25 minutes **cooking time** 10 minutes **serves** 4

2 pounds cooked medium shrimp

7 ounces snow peas, trimmed,
sliced thinly

1 bunch fresh chives, cut into
1 ½-inch lengths

2 cups baby spinach

1 medium avocado, sliced thickly

Ginger dressing

5-inch piece fresh ginger, grated

3 tablespoons olive oil

3 tablespoons freh lemon juice

1 teaspoon sugar

1 Peel and devein shrimp; cut shrimp in half lengthwise.

2 Make ginger dressing.

3 Place shrimp in large bowl with snow peas, chives, spinach, avocado and
dressing; toss gently to combine.

Ginger dressing Press grated ginger between two spoons over mixing bowl;
discard fibers. Add remaining ingredients; whisk until well combined.

NUTRITIONAL INFO PER SERVING 20g total fat (4g saturated fat);
5g carbohydrate; 29g protein; 4g fiber; 318 calories

salade niçoise

preparation time 20 minutes **cooking time** 10 minutes **serves** 4

7 ounces green beans, trimmed,
  chopped coarsely
8 ounces cherry tomatoes, halved
½ cup pitted black olives
2 small cucumbers, sliced thickly
1 medium red onion, sliced thinly
3 cups mixed salad greens
6 hard-boiled eggs, quartered
15 ounces canned tuna, drained

Vinaigrette
1 teaspoon olive oil
¼ cup fresh lemon juice
1 clove garlic, crushed
2 teaspoons Dijon mustard

1 Boil, steam or microwave beans until just tender; drain. Rinse under cold water; drain.

2 Make vinaigrette.

3 Place tomatoes, olives, cucumbers, onion, salad greens and eggs in large bowl with vinaigrette; toss gently to combine. Divide salad among serving plates; flake tuna over salad in large chunks.

Vinaigrette Whisk together all ingredients.

NUTRITIONAL INFO PER SERVING 11g total fat (3g saturated fat); 11g carbohydrate; 31g protein; 5g fiber; 269 calories

roasted pear, Belgian endive and spinach salad

preparation time 10 minutes **cooking time** 25 minutes **serves** 4

6 ripe Bartlett or Bosc pears
  (about 1 ¼ pounds)
2 teaspoons sugar
6 fresh medium figs
6 heads Belgian endive (about 1 ¾ pounds)
7 ounces baby spinach
⅔ cup roasted walnuts, chopped coarsely
1 ½ tablespoons white wine vinegar
¼ cup fresh orange juice
½ cup olive oil
1 clove garlic, crushed
3 ½ ounces gorgonzola cheese,
  chopped finely

1 Preheat oven to 350°F.

2 Quarter and core pears; place in large lightly oiled deep baking dish. Sprinkle pears with sugar; bake, uncovered, about 25 minutes or until tender, turning halfway through baking time.

3 Cut figs into wedges. Separate endive leaves. Place figs and endive in large serving bowl with spinach and walnuts.

4 Whisk together vinegar, orange juice, oil and garlic. Add pears, cheese and dressing to salad; toss gently to combine.

Tip Roasted pears and dressing can be made a day ahead, but it is best not to assemble this salad until just before serving.

NUTRITIONAL INFO PER SERVING 50g total fat (10g saturated fat); 31g carbohydrate; 13g protein; 11g fiber; 643 calories

chicken chowder

preparation time 15 minutes **cooking time** 40 minutes **serves** 4

2 cups chicken stock

2 cups water

14 ounces boneless, skinless
   chicken breasts

3 tablespoons butter

3-4 slices bacon (5 ounces),
   chopped coarsely

1 medium onion, chopped finely

1 clove garlic, crushed

1 medium leek, sliced thinly

1 celery stalk, chopped finely

¼ cup all-purpose flour

2 medium potatoes, chopped coarsely

1 quart (4 cups) milk

½ cup heavy cream

3 tablespoons finely chopped fresh chives

1 Bring stock and the water to a boil in medium pot; add chicken, return to a boil. Reduce heat; simmer, covered, about 10 minutes or until chicken is cooked through. Cool chicken in poaching liquid 10 minutes. Remove chicken from pot; discard poaching liquid (or keep for another use). Shred chicken coarsely.

2 Heat butter in large pot; cook bacon, onion, garlic, leek and celery, stirring, until vegetables soften.

3 Stir in flour; cook, stirring, 1 minute. Stir in potatoes, milk and cream; simmer, covered, about 15 minutes or until potatoes are just tender.

4 Add chicken and chives: cook, stirring, until heated through.

NUTRITIONAL INFO PER SERVING 37g total fat (23g saturated fat); 36g carbohydrate; 42g protein; 5g fiber; 651 calories

pizza sandwich supreme

preparation time 10 minutes   **cooking time** 10 minutes   **serves** 4

1 ½ tablespoons olive oil

2 cloves garlic, crushed

1 small red onion, sliced thinly

1 small green bell pepper, sliced thinly

2 ounces cremini mushrooms, sliced thinly

1 long loaf focaccia or ciabatta

¼ cup tomato paste

4 ounces hot salami, sliced thinly

3 ounces marinated artichoke hearts,
   drained, sliced thinly

3 ½ ounces fresh mozzarella cheese,
   sliced thickly

1 Heat oil in large skillet; cook garlic and onion, stirring, until onion softens. Add bell pepper and mushrooms; cook, stirring, until mushrooms soften.

2 Preheat sandwich press. Cut bread crosswise into four pieces; split each piece horizontally.

3 Spread tomato paste evenly over four pieces of bread, then top with equal amounts of vegetable mixture, salami, artichoke and cheese. Top with remaining bread.

4 Toast sandwiches in heated sandwich press.

Tip You can make these sandwiches in a heated oiled skillet. Cover with another heavy skillet while cooking to press sandwich down.

NUTRITIONAL INFO PER SERVING 23g total fat (7g saturated fat); 53g carbohydrate; 23g protein; 5g fiber; 523 calories

grilled scallops with papaya salsa

preparation time 15 minutes **cooking time** 10 minutes **serves** 4

1 ¾ pounds firm papaya,
   chopped coarsely
2 medium tomatoes, seeded,
   chopped coarsely
1 medium red onion, chopped coarsely
¼ cup fresh lime juice
1 fresh small red serrano or Thai chili,
   seeded, chopped finely (optional)
3 tablespoons coarsely chopped
   fresh cilantro
1 ½ tablespoons vegetable oil
36 sea scallops

1 Combine papaya, tomatoes, onion, lime juice, chili, cilantro and oil in large bowl.
2 Cook scallops on heated oiled grill pan, in batches, until browned.
3 Serve papaya salsa topped with scallops.

NUTRITIONAL INFO PER SERVING 6g total fat (1g saturated fat);
15g carbohydrate; 27g protein; 5g fiber; 239 calories

chicken tacos with guacamole and fresh salsa

preparation time 20 minutes **cooking time** 15 minutes **serves** 4

2 teaspoons chili powder

2 medium avocados (1 pound)

¼ cup sour cream

3 tablespoons fresh lime juice

3 tablespoons vegetable oil

2 teaspoons ground cumin

2 teaspoons ground coriander

2 pounds chicken tenders

8 large flour tortillas

1 cup coarsely grated cheddar cheese

Fresh salsa

4 medium plum tomatoes, seeded, chopped finely

¼ cup bottled jalapeño peppers, rinsed, drained, chopped finely

¼ cup coarsely chopped fresh cilantro

1 medium avocado, chopped coarsely

1½ tablespoons fresh lime juice

1 Preheat broiler.

2 Combine chili powder, avocados, sour cream and lime juice in medium bowl; mash roughly with fork.

3 Combine oil and spices in large bowl, add chicken; mix well. Cook chicken on heated oiled grill pan, in batches, until cooked.

4 Make fresh salsa.

5 Divide chicken and avocado mixture among tortillas; fold to enclose filling.

6 Place tacos on baking sheet; sprinkle with cheese. Broil until cheese melts and is golden brown. Serve with salsa.

Fresh salsa Combine ingredients in medium bowl.

NUTRITIONAL INFO PER SERVING 81g total fat (25g saturated fat); 45g carbohydrate; 66g protein; 6g fiber; 1181 calories

chicken and leek puff pastry squares

preparation time 20 minutes (plus cooling time)   **cooking time** 25 minutes   **serves** 4

3 tablespoons butter

1 small leek, sliced thinly

2 cloves garlic, crushed

1 pound boneless, skinless chicken
   breasts, chopped coarsely

3 tablespoons cornstarch

½ cup dry white wine

½ cup chicken stock

½ cup heavy cream

2 sheets frozen puff pastry, thawed

1 egg, beaten lightly

1 Preheat oven to 400°F.

2 Melt butter in large skillet; cook leek and garlic, stirring, until leek softens. Add chicken; cook, stirring, until chicken is browned lightly.

3 Add blended cornstarch and wine, then stock and cream; stir until mixture boils and thickens. Reduce heat; simmer, uncovered, 5 minutes. Spread onto baking sheet; cool 10 minutes.

4 Cut each pastry sheet in half; place pastry pieces on greased baking sheets. Spoon a quarter of the chicken mixture onto half of one piece, leaving ½-inch border; brush edges with egg. Fold pastry over to enclose filling; pinch edges together tightly to seal. Cut two slits in top of pastry square; brush with egg. Repeat with remaining pastry, chicken mixture and egg. Bake, uncovered, about 15 minutes or until just browned.

Tip Uncooked pies can be frozen, covered tightly, for up to a month. Thaw overnight in the refrigerator before baking.

NUTRITIONAL INFO PER SERVING 49g total fat (27g saturated fat); 37g carbohydrate; 32g protein; 2g fiber; 734 calories

falafel burgers

preparation time 15 minutes **cooking time** 10 minutes **serves** 4

A snack eaten throughout the Middle East and North Africa, falafels are small patties made of crushed fried chickpeas or beans and a variety of herbs.

two 10 ½-ounce cans chickpeas,
  rinsed, drained
1 medium onion, chopped coarsely
2 cloves garlic, quartered
½ cup coarsely chopped fresh
  flat-leaf parsley
2 teaspoons ground coriander
1 teaspoon ground cumin
1 teaspoon baking soda
3 tablespoons all-purpose flour
1 egg, beaten lightly
1 large flatbread
1 large tomato, sliced thinly
1 cup arugula

Yogurt and tahini sauce
¼ cup yogurt
3 tablespoons tahini
1 ½ tablespoons fresh lemon juice

1 Blend or process chickpeas, onion, garlic, parsley, coriander, cumin, baking soda, flour and egg until almost smooth. Shape mixture by hand into four burgers. Cook burgers on heated oiled griddle or skillet, uncovered, about 5 minutes or until browned on one side. Turn carefully, using two spatulas, and cook the other side for 5 minutes, or until browned.

2 Cut bread into quarters; toast on both sides on heated oiled grill or grill pan.

3 Make yogurt and tahini sauce.

4 Split each piece of bread in half horizontally; layer sauce, tomato, burgers and arugula between bread halves.

Yogurt and tahini sauce Combine ingredients in small bowl.

NUTRITIONAL INFO PER SERVING 14g total fat (21g saturated fat); 70g carbohydrate; 23g protein; 11g fiber; 523 calories

tomato leek frittata with spinach salad

preparation time 15 minutes **cooking time** 25 minutes **serves** 4

You'll need a medium skillet with an 8-inch base for this recipe.

6 eggs
½ cup light evaporated milk
1 ½ tablespoons butter
1 medium leek, sliced thinly
⅔ cup frozen peas
2 medium tomatoes, sliced thinly
3 tablespoons finely grated
  parmesan cheese
3 cups baby spinach
8 ounces yellow or red grape tomatoes,
  halved
½ small red onion, sliced thinly
2 teaspoons olive oil
1 teaspoon red wine vinegar

1 Preheat broiler.
2 Combine eggs and milk in large bowl.
3 Heat butter in medium broiler-safe skillet; cook leek, stirring, until softened. Add peas, sliced tomatoes and egg mixture; cook, uncovered, over low heat until frittata is almost set. Remove from heat; sprinkle with cheese.
4 Place under broiler until frittata sets and top is browned lightly. Let frittata stand in pan 5 minutes before cutting into wedges.
5 Place remaining ingredients in medium bowl; toss gently to combine.
6 Serve frittata with salad.

NUTRITIONAL INFO PER SERVING 16g total fat (6g saturated fat); 11g carbohydrate; 18g protein; 5g fiber; 258 calories

Thai chicken noodle soup

preparation time 15 minutes **cooking time** 15 minutes **serves** 4

4 cups chicken stock

2 cups water

1-inch piece fresh ginger, grated

1 fresh small red serrano or Thai chili,
   chopped finely (optional)

¾ pound chicken breast fillets,
   sliced thinly

12 ounces fresh rice noodles or
   3 ounces dried rice noodles

1 tablespoon fish sauce

1 tablespoon palm sugar or brown sugar

1 tablespoon fresh lime juice

2 baby bok choy, quartered

⅓ cup loosely packed fresh basil leaves

1 Combine stock, water, ginger and chili in large pot; cover, and bring to a boil. Reduce heat; simmer 5 minutes. Add chicken, noodles, fish sauce, sugar and lime juice; simmer about 5 minutes or until chicken is cooked through and noodles are tender.

2 Divide bok choy among serving bowls; ladle chicken mixture into bowls. Sprinkle with basil.

NUTRITIONAL INFO PER SERVING 7g total fat (2g saturated fat); 28g carbohydrate; 28g protein; 2g fiber; 289 calories

smoked salmon and avocado salad

preparation time 20 minutes **serves** 4

3 cups mixed salad greens

1 pound smoked salmon, sliced thinly

2 medium avocados (about 1 pound),
   chopped coarsely

1 medium red onion, sliced thinly

9 ounces goat cheese, crumbled

3 tablespoons finely chopped fresh dill

⅓ cup fresh lemon juice

1 ½ tablespoons Dijon mustard

3 tablespoons honey

2 cloves garlic, crushed

1 ½ tablespoons white vinegar

1 ½ tablespoons olive oil

1 Combine salad greens, salmon, avocados, onion and goat cheese in large bowl.

2 Whisk remaining ingredients in small bowl then pour over salad; toss gently
to combine.

NUTRITIONAL INFO PER SERVING 39g total fat (12g saturated fat);
17g carbohydrate; 40g protein; 3g fiber; 578 calories

chicken tandoori wraps with raita

preparation time 10 minutes **cooking time** 10 minutes **makes** 8

1 ½ tablespoons fresh lime juice
⅓ cup tandoori paste
¼ cup yogurt
14 ounces chicken tenders
8 large flour tortillas
2 ounces fresh bean sprouts

Raita
1 cup yogurt
1 small cucumber, halved, seeded, chopped finely
1 ½ tablespoons finely chopped fresh mint

1 Combine lime juice, tandoori paste and yogurt in medium bowl; add chicken, toss to coat chicken in marinade.

2 Cook chicken, in batches, on heated oiled grill or grill pan until cooked through. Let stand 5 minutes; slice thickly.

3 Heat tortillas on same heated oiled grill or grill pan for 1 minute each side or until softened.

4 Place equal amounts of each of the chicken, sprouts and raita on a quarter section of each tortilla; fold tortilla in half and then in half again to enclose filling and form triangle-shaped pockets.

Raita Combine ingredients in small bowl.

NUTRITIONAL INFO PER SERVING 8g total fat (2g saturated fat); 5g carbohydrate; 14g protein; 2g fiber; 155 calories

Pasta

Quite possibly everyone's favorite quick fix, pasta satisfies all the senses. Get creative with fresh new combinations or enjoy a comforting classic.

penne puttanesca

preparation time 10 minutes **cooking time** 20 minutes **serves** 4

1 pound penne pasta

⅓ cup extra virgin olive oil

3 cloves garlic, crushed

1 teaspoon crushed red pepper flakes

5 medium tomatoes (about 2 pounds), chopped coarsely

7 ounces pitted Kalamata olives

8 drained anchovy fillets, chopped coarsely

⅓ cup drained capers, rinsed

⅓ cup coarsely chopped fresh flat-leaf parsley

3 tablespoons finely shredded fresh basil

1 Cook pasta in large pot of boiling salted water, uncovered, until just tender.

2 Heat oil in large skillet; cook garlic, stirring, until fragrant. Add crushed red pepper and tomatoes; cook, stirring, 5 minutes. Add remaining ingredients; cook, stirring occasionally, about 5 minutes or until sauce thickens slightly.

3 Add drained pasta to puttanesca sauce; toss gently to combine.

NUTRITIONAL INFO PER SERVING 21g total fat (3g saturated fat); 102g carbohydrate; 19g protein; 8g fiber; 690 calories

fettucine with chicken and mushroom cream sauce

preparation time 10 minutes **cooking time** 10 minutes **serves** 4

1 pound fettucine

1½ tablespoons olive oil

1 medium onion, chopped finely

3 slices bacon (5 ounces), chopped finely

7 ounces button mushrooms, sliced finely

¼ cup dry white wine

⅔ cup heavy cream

1 cup milk

1 cup thinly sliced cooked chicken

¼ cup finely grated parmesan cheese

3 tablespoons coarsely chopped fresh
   flat-leaf parsley or basil

1 Cook pasta in large pot of boiling salted water, uncovered, until just tender; drain, reserving ½ cup of cooking liquid.

2 Heat oil in large pot; cook onion, stirring, until soft. Add bacon and mushrooms; cook, stirring, 1 minute.

3 Add wine, cream and milk; bring to a boil. Reduce heat; simmer, stirring, 5 minutes. Add chicken; stir until combined.

4 Add pasta, cheese, parsley and reserved cooking liquid; toss gently over low heat until hot.

NUTRITIONAL INFO PER SERVING 36g total fat (18g saturated fat); 95g carbohydrate; 43g protein; 8g fiber; 898 calories

spaghetti with mussels and clams

preparation time 15 minutes   **cooking time** 15 minutes   **serves** 4

1 pound mussels

1 pound clams

¼ cup water

¼ cup dry white wine

1 pound spaghetti

⅓ cup extra virgin olive oil

2 cloves garlic, crushed

1 small red serrano or Thai chili,
   chopped finely (optional)

2 medium tomatoes, seeded,
   chopped coarsely

½ cup coarsely chopped fresh
   flat-leaf parsley

1 Scrub mussels; remove beards. Rinse clams.

2 Combine the water and wine in large pot; bring to a boil. Add mussels and clams; reduce heat, simmer, covered, about 5 minutes or until mussels open (discard any that do not). Strain cooking liquid through fine sieve into medium bowl; reserve ⅓ cup, discard remainder. Strain remaining ⅓ cup of the cooking liquid again, into small cup. Cover mussels and clams to keep warm.

3 Cook pasta in large pot of boiling salted water, uncovered, until just tender.

4 Heat oil in large skillet; cook garlic and chili, stirring, until fragrant. Add tomatoes and reserved cooking liquid; bring to a boil.

5 Place drained pasta, mussels, clams and tomato mixture in large bowl with parsley; toss gently to combine.

NUTRITIONAL INFO PER SERVING 20g total fat (3g saturated fat); 89g carbohydrate; 23g protein; 6g fiber; 652 calories

farfalle with chicken, spinach and tomato

preparation time 15 minutes **cooking time** 10 minutes **serves** 4

12 ounces farfalle pasta

1 ½ tablespoons olive oil

1 medium onion, chopped finely

1 clove garlic, crushed

1 ¼ pounds chicken tenders,
    chopped coarsely

5 cups baby spinach

1 cup ricotta cheese

1 egg

2 teaspoons finely grated lemon peel

3 tablespoons fresh lemon juice

7 ounces grape tomatoes, halved

¼ cup finely grated parmesan cheese

1 Cook pasta in large pot of boiling salted water, uncovered, until just tender; drain.

2 Heat oil in large deep skillet; cook onion and garlic, stirring, until onion softens. Add chicken; cook, stirring, over medium heat, about 5 minutes or until cooked through.

3 Place chicken mixture, spinach, combined ricotta and egg, lemon peel, lemon juice, tomatoes and drained pasta in large serving bowl; toss gently to combine.

4 Serve sprinkled with grated parmesan.

Tip Farfalle are short, sturdy, butterfly-shaped pasta that look like bow ties. They are great in dishes like these because they help hold the other ingredients. You can replace the farfalle with penne or shells.

NUTRITIONAL INFO PER SERVING 21g total fat (8g saturated fat); 68g carbohydrate; 52g protein; 6g fiber; 682 calories

spicy sausage pasta bake

preparation time 15 minutes **cooking time** 35 minutes **serves** 6

12 ounces rigatoni or ziti pasta

2 pounds spicy Italian sausage

1 medium onion, chopped coarsely

1 small eggplant, chopped coarsely

2 medium red bell peppers,
  chopped coarsely

3 small green zucchini, chopped coarsely

26-ounce jar pasta sauce

½ cup coarsely chopped fresh basil

2 cups grated mozzarella cheese

1 Preheat oven to 350°F.

2 Cook pasta in large pot of boiling salted water, uncovered, until just tender; drain.

3 Cook sausage in large non-stick skillet until just cooked through. Drain on paper towels.

4 Cook onion, eggplant, bell peppers and zucchini, stirring, in same skillet until just tender.

5 Cut sausages into ¾-inch slices; add to vegetables in skillet with sauce and basil, stir to combine.

6 Combine pasta and sausage mixture in deep 3-quart casserole dish; sprinkle with cheese. Bake, uncovered, about 20 minutes or until browned lightly.

NUTRITIONAL INFO PER SERVING 36g total fat (17g saturated fat); 68g carbohydrate; 58g protein; 8g fiber; 826 calories

linguine with shrimp, peas, lemon and dill

preparation time 10 minutes **cooking time** 20 minutes **serves** 4

2 pounds uncooked large shrimp

12 ounces linguine

3 tablespoons olive oil

2 cloves garlic, crushed

1 ½ cups frozen peas

2 teaspoons finely grated lemon peel

6 green onions, sliced thinly

1 ½ tablespoons coarsely chopped
   fresh dill

¼ cup fresh lemon juice

1 Peel and devein shrimp; halve lengthwise.

2 Cook pasta in large pot of boiling salted water, uncovered, until just tender; drain. Return to pot.

3 Heat half of the oil in large skillet; cook garlic and shrimp, in batches, until shrimp are just changed in color. Cover to keep warm.

4 Place peas in same skillet; cook, stirring, until heated through. Add lemon peel, onions and dill; cook, stirring, until onions are just tender. Return shrimp to skillet with lemon juice; stir until heated through. Add shrimp mixture and remaining oil to hot pasta; toss gently to combine.

NUTRITIONAL INFO PER SERVING 16g total fat (2g saturated fat); 70g carbohydrate; 39g protein; 8g fiber; 584 calories

chicken and pecan pasta salad

preparation time 15 minutes **cooking time** 15 minutes **serves** 4

1 pound farfalle pasta

3 tablespoons warm water

½ cup sour cream

½ cup mayonnaise

1 ½ tablespoons Dijon mustard

3 cups (1 pound) shredded cooked chicken

2 celery stalks, sliced thinly

1 cup (1 ½ ounces) roasted pecans,
   halved lengthwise

1 small red onion, sliced thinly

1 Cook pasta in large pot of boiling salted water, uncovered, until just tender; drain. Rinse under cold water; drain.

2 Combine the water, sour cream, mayonnaise and mustard in large bowl. Add pasta and remaining ingredients to bowl; toss gently to combine.

Tip You'll need to purchase a large rotisserie chicken weighing approximately 2 pounds for this recipe.

NUTRITIONAL INFO PER SERVING 55g total fat (14g saturated fat); 97g carbohydrate; 48g protein; 8g fiber; 1093 calories

linguine with pesto, beans and potatoes

preparation time 25 minutes **cooking time** 10 minutes **serves** 4

This is the true pasta with pesto from Italy's Ligurian coast. The potatoes soak up the flavorful oil from the pesto and the beans add a sweet, delightful crunch to the dish.

8 ounces green beans,
   cut into 2-inch lengths
2 medium potatoes (14 ounces),
   sliced thinly lengthwise
1 pound linguine
3 ½-ounce piece romano cheese, shaved

Basil pesto
1 cup firmly packed fresh basil
¼ cup finely grated romano cheese
¼ cup toasted pine nuts
2 cloves garlic, crushed
½ cup olive oil

1 Blend or process basil pesto ingredients until mixture forms a coarse paste.

2 Boil, steam or microwave beans and potatoes, separately, until just tender; drain.

3 Cook pasta in large pot of boiling salted water, uncovered, until just tender; drain, reserving ½-cup cooking liquid.

4 Combine beans, potatoes and pasta in large bowl. Stir reserved liquid into pesto; pour over pasta. Add cheese; toss gently to combine.

NUTRITIONAL INFO PER SERVING 45g total fat (10g saturated fat); 101g carbohydrate; 27g protein; 10g fiber; 925 calories

warm pasta provençale salad

preparation time 15 minutes **cooking time** 15 minutes **serves** 6

12 ounces rigatoni pasta

1 ¼ pounds boneless leg of lamb

¾ cup pitted black olives, halved

1 cup drained sun-dried tomatoes in oil, coarsely chopped

14 ½-ounce can artichoke hearts, drained and halved

1 small red onion, sliced thinly

2 ounces baby arugula leaves

½ cup green or black olive tapenade

2 tablespoons olive oil

2 tablespoons fresh lemon juice

1 Cook pasta in large pot of boiling salted water until tender; drain.

2 Sauté lamb, uncovered, in large skillet until desired degree of doneness. Cover; let stand 5 minutes, and slice into thick pieces.

3 Combine pasta with lamb and remaining ingredients in large bowl. Serve warm.

NUTRITIONAL INFO PER SERVING 17g total fat (3g saturated fat); 57g carbohydrate; 32g protein; 8g fiber; 527 calories

ricotta and spinach ravioli with pumpkin sauce

preparation time 10 minutes **cooking time** 25 minutes **serves** 4

¼ cup olive oil

1 small onion, chopped finely

1 clove garlic, crushed

1 ¼ pounds pumpkin or butternut squash,
   sliced thinly

1 ½ cups chicken stock

½ teaspoon ground nutmeg

½ cup heavy cream

½ cup hot water

1 ¼ pounds fresh spinach and
   ricotta ravioli

⅓ cup toasted pine nuts

3 tablespoons coarsely chopped
   fresh chives

1 Heat half of the oil in large skillet; cook onion and garlic, stirring, until onion softens. Remove from skillet.

2 Heat remaining oil in same skillet; cook pumpkin, in batches, until browned lightly. Return pumpkin and onion mixture to skillet with stock and nutmeg; cook, stirring, until liquid is absorbed. Blend or process pumpkin mixture with cream and the hot water until smooth. Return to skillet; stir, over low heat, until heated through.

3 Cook ravioli in pot of boiling salted water, uncovered, until just tender; drain.

4 Serve pasta with pumpkin sauce, sprinkled with nuts and chives.

NUTRITIONAL INFO PER SERVING 42g total fat (14g saturated fat); 32g carbohydrate; 18g protein; 5g fiber; 572 calories

spaghetti with garlic and breadcrumbs

preparation time 10 minutes **cooking time** 10 minutes **serves** 4

12 ounces spaghetti

⅓ cup olive oil

4 tablespoons butter

4 cloves garlic, crushed

1 teaspoon crushed red pepper flakes
   (optional)

2 cups dried breadcrumbs

½ cup coarsely chopped fresh
   flat-leaf parsley

2 teaspoons finely grated lemon peel

1 Cook pasta in large pot of boiling salted water, uncovered, until just tender.

2 Heat half of the oil in skillet with butter. After butter melts, add garlic, red pepper and breadcrumbs; cook, stirring, until breadcrumbs are browned lightly.

3 Combine drained hot pasta and breadcrumb mixture in large bowl with parsley, lemon peel and remaining oil.

NUTRITIONAL INFO PER SERVING 31g total fat (10g saturated fat); 88g carbohydrate; 16g protein; 6g fiber; 707 calories

fettucine with sausage and tomato cream sauce

preparation time 10 minutes **cooking time** 30 minutes **serves** 4

cooking-oil spray

1 pound Italian sausage

2 cloves garlic, crushed

14 ½-ounce can crushed tomatoes, undrained

¼ cup dry white wine

1 ½ cups heavy cream

12 ounces fettucine

6 green onions, chopped finely

3 tablespoons fresh sage

1 Lightly spray large skillet with oil; cook sausages until browned all over and cooked through. Remove sausages from skillet; chop coarsely. Cover to keep warm. Drain excess oil from skillet.

2 Combine garlic, undrained tomatoes, wine and cream in skillet; bring to a boil. Reduce heat; simmer, uncovered, about 10 minutes or until sauce thickens slightly.

3 Cook pasta in large pot of boiling salted water, uncovered, until just tender; drain. Divide among serving bowls.

4 Stir sausage with onions and sage into tomato mixture; spoon sauce over pasta.

NUTRITIONAL INFO PER SERVING 62g total fat (35g saturated fat); 75g carbohydrate; 30g protein; 7g fiber; 992 calories

gnocchi with spinach cream sauce

preparation time 10 minutes **cooking time** 15 minutes **serves** 4

1 ¼ pounds fresh gnocchi

2 tablespoons butter

1 medium onion, chopped finely

1 clove garlic, crushed

½ cup dry white wine

¾ cup heavy cream

¾ cup vegetable or chicken stock

10 ½ cups baby spinach,
   shredded coarsely

½ cup finely grated parmesan cheese

1 Cook gnocchi in large pot of boiling salted water, uncovered, about 5 minutes or until gnocchi float to the surface; drain.

2 Melt butter in large pot; cook onion and garlic, stirring, until onion softens. Stir in wine, cream and stock; bring to a boil. Boil, uncovered, 2 minutes.

3 Add spinach and cheese; cook, stirring, until spinach is just wilted and cheese melts. Serve gnocchi topped with spinach cream sauce.

NUTRITIONAL INFO PER SERVING 31g total fat (20g saturated fat); 48g carbohydrate; 14g protein; 6g fiber; 555 calories

penne with grilled vegetables and sun-dried tomato mayonnaise

preparation time 10 minutes **cooking time** 20 minutes **serves** 4

12 ounces penne pasta

5 baby yellow squash (about 12 ounces), halved crosswise

2 medium zucchini, sliced thinly

12 ounces asparagus, trimmed, cut into 2-inch lengths

2 baby eggplants, sliced thinly

1 small red onion, cut into wedges

8 ounces cherry tomatoes

1 medium red bell pepper, sliced thickly

½ cup mayonnaise

1 ½ tablespoons sun-dried tomato pesto or 1 ½ tablespoons finely minced sun-dried tomatoes in oil

1 Cook pasta in large pot of boiling salted water, uncovered, until just tender; drain.

2 Cook vegetables on heated oiled grill or grill pan, uncovered, until just tender.

3 Combine mayonnaise and pesto in large bowl. Add pasta and vegetables; toss gently to combine.

NUTRITIONAL INFO PER SERVING 16g total fat (2g saturated fat); 80g carbohydrate; 16g protein; 9g fiber; 544 calories

creamy farfalle with fried zucchini

preparation time 10 minutes **cooking time** 20 minutes **serves** 4

12 ounces farfalle pasta

3 tablespoons olive oil

3 cloves garlic, crushed

6 small zucchini, grated coarsely

2 teaspoons finely grated lemon peel

1 ½ tablespoons finely chopped fresh
   flat-leaf parsley

3 green onions, sliced thinly

½ cup finely grated parmesan cheese

1 ½ cups heavy cream

1 Cook pasta in large pot of boiling salted water, uncovered, until just tender.

2 Heat oil in large skillet; cook garlic, stirring, about 2 minutes or until fragrant.
Add zucchini; cook, stirring, 2 minutes.

3 Combine lemon peel, parsley, onions and cheese in small bowl.

4 Add cream and drained hot pasta to zucchini mixture; stir gently over low heat
until heated through. Serve pasta immediately, topped with cheese mixture.

NUTRITIONAL INFO PER SERVING 46g total fat (25g saturated fat);
69g carbohydrate; 18g protein; 6g fiber; 772 calories

rigatoni with bacon and asparagus

preparation time 15 minutes **cooking time** 25 minutes **serves** 4

1 pound rigatoni pasta

1 pound asparagus, chopped coarsely

8 slices bacon (12 ounces), sliced thinly

1 clove garlic, crushed

4 tablespoons butter, chopped

½ cup freshly grated parmesan cheese

½ cup finely shredded mozzarella cheese

⅓ cup heavy cream

¼ cup coarsely chopped fresh
   flat-leaf parsley

1 Cook pasta in large pot of boiling salted water, uncovered, until just tender.

2 Boil, steam or microwave asparagus until just tender; drain.

3 Cook bacon in large heated non-stick skillet, stirring, until crisp. Add garlic; cook, stirring, until fragrant.

4 Place drained pasta, asparagus and bacon mixture in large bowl with butter, cheeses and cream; toss gently to combine. Serve pasta sprinkled with parsley.

NUTRITIONAL INFO PER SERVING 31g total fat (18g saturated fat); 90g carbohydrate; 33g protein; 8g fiber; 775 calories

rigatoni bolognese

preparation time 5 minutes **cooking time** 30 minutes **serves** 4

1 medium onion, chopped coarsely

1 large carrot, chopped coarsely

1 celery stalk, chopped coarsely

1 ½ tablespoons olive oil

4 tablespoons butter

2 cloves garlic, crushed

6 ounces bulk Italian sausage

1 pound ground beef and pork

3 tablespoons tomato paste

½ cup dry white wine

¼ cup beef stock

14 ½-ounce can crushed tomatoes,
   undrained

3 tablespoons finely chopped fresh basil

3 tablespoons finely chopped fresh
   flat-leaf parsley

1 pound rigatoni pasta

¼ cup freshly grated parmesan cheese

1 Blend or process onion, carrot and celery until chopped finely.

2 Heat oil and butter in large pot, cook onion mixture and garlic, stirring occasionally, 5 minutes.

3 Add sausage and ground meat to pot; cook, stirring, until meats are browned.

4 Stir in tomato paste and wine; bring to a boil. Reduce heat; simmer, uncovered, 2 minutes. Add stock and tomatoes; return to a boil. Reduce heat; simmer, uncovered, about 20 minutes or until bolognese thickens. Stir in herbs.

5 Cook pasta in pot of boiling salted water, uncovered, until just tender; drain.

6 Serve pasta topped with bolognese and sprinkled with cheese.

NUTRITIONAL INFO PER SERVING 37g total fat (17g saturated fat); 97g carbohydrate; 49g protein; 10g fiber; 941 calories

angel hair with peas and ricotta

preparation time 15 minutes **cooking time** 15 minutes **serves** 4

12 ounces angel hair pasta

5 ounces sugar snap peas, trimmed

5 ounces snow peas, trimmed

½ cup frozen peas

1 ½ tablespoons olive oil

1 medium red onion, sliced thinly

2 cloves garlic, crushed

3 tablespoons drained baby capers, rinsed

½ cup fresh lemon juice

½ cup coarsely chopped fresh mint

½ cup coarsely chopped fresh
   flat-leaf parsley

7 ounces low-fat ricotta cheese, crumbled

1 Cook pasta in large pot of boiling salted water, uncovered, until just tender; drain.

2 Boil, steam or microwave peas until just tender; drain. Rinse under cold water; drain.

3 Heat oil in large pot; cook onion, garlic and capers, stirring, 2 minutes. Add pasta; cook, stirring, 3 minutes. Place pasta mixture, peas, lemon juice and herbs in large bowl; toss gently.

4 Serve pasta topped with cheese.

NUTRITIONAL INFO PER SERVING 10g total fat (4g saturated fat); 74g carbohydrate; 20g protein; 8g fiber; 476 calories

fettucine with grilled vegetables and basil tapenade

preparation time 20 minutes **cooking time** 25 minutes **serves** 4

1 large eggplant (about 1 pound),
 sliced thickly
2 large zucchini, sliced thickly
8 ounces cherry tomatoes
12 ounces fettucine
1 cup loosely packed fresh basil

Basil tapenade
2 ½ cups pitted black olives
3 tablespoons drained capers, rinsed
1 clove garlic, quartered
3 tablespoons fresh lemon juice
¼ cup loosely packed fresh basil
⅓ cup olive oil

1 Make basil tapenade.
2 Cook eggplant, zucchini and tomatoes, in batches, on heated oiled grill or grill pan until browned.
3 Cook pasta in pot of boiling salted water, uncovered, until just tender; drain.
4 Place pasta in medium bowl with vegetables, tapenade and basil; toss gently to combine.

Basil tapenade Blend or process ingredients until smooth.

Tip Making the tapenade using a mortar and pestle will give it a lovely, thick texture. Try stirring a spoonful of tapenade into a pasta sauce or vegetable soup, spreading it on a slice of bruschetta, or thinning it with mayonnaise for a dip.

NUTRITIONAL INFO PER SERVING 21g total fat (3g saturated fat); 89g carbohydrate; 14g protein; 11g fiber; 599 calories

four-cheese pasta bake

preparation time 20 minutes **cooking time** 30 minutes **serves** 6

1 pound penne pasta

4 green onions, chopped finely

½ cup drained sun-dried tomatoes, chopped coarsely

3 tablespoons olive oil

2 cloves garlic, crushed

¼ cup coarsely chopped fresh basil

½ loaf flatbread or large round pita bread, diced into ½-inch pieces

Four-cheese sauce

4 tablespoons butter

⅓ cup all-purpose flour

1 quart (4 cups) milk

⅓ cup finely grated fontina cheese

¾ cup finely grated mozzarella cheese

¾ cup finely grated parmesan cheese

3 ½ ounces gorgonzola cheese, crumbled

1 Preheat oven to 350°F. Lightly grease deep 3-quart baking dish.

2 Cook pasta in large pot of boiling salted water until just tender.

3 Make four-cheese sauce.

4 Drain pasta; return to same pot with onions, tomatoes and cheese sauce; toss gently to combine. Transfer pasta mixture to baking dish.

5 Combine oil, garlic and basil in medium bowl; add bread, toss gently to combine topping mixture.

6 Sprinkle topping mixture over pasta bake in even layer; cook, uncovered, about 15 minutes or until topping is browned lightly and pasta bake is cooked through.

7 Serve pasta with a spinach and parmesan salad, if desired.

Four-cheese sauce Melt butter in medium pot, add flour; cook, stirring, until mixture bubbles and thickens. Gradually add milk; cook, stirring, until sauce boils and thickens. Remove from heat, add cheeses; stir until smooth.

NUTRITIONAL INFO PER SERVING 39g total fat (18g saturated fat); 88g carbohydrate; 36g protein; 7g fiber; 891 calories

spaghetti and meatballs

preparation time 20 minutes **cooking time** 20 minutes **serves** 4

We've made twice the number of meatballs required to serve four; freeze half of the meatballs for future use, when time is short.

2 pounds ground beef

1 small green bell pepper, chopped finely

1 small onion, chopped finely

4 cloves garlic, crushed

¼ cup coarsely chopped fresh
   flat-leaf parsley

1 egg

1 cup breadcrumbs

1 teaspoon finely grated lemon peel

½ cup sun-dried tomato pesto

3 tablespoons olive oil

1 medium onion, sliced thinly

½ cup dry red wine

2 cups pasta sauce

½ cup chicken stock

¼ cup coarsely chopped fresh basil

12 ounces spaghetti

⅓ cup shaved parmesan cheese

1 Combine beef, bell pepper, chopped onion, 2 cloves of garlic, parsley, egg, breadcrumbs, lemon peel and pesto by hand in large bowl; roll heaping tablespoons of beef mixture into balls.

2 Heat oil in large skillet; cook meatballs, in batches, until browned all over. Drain on paper towels.

3 Cook 2 other cloves of garlic and sliced onion in same skillet, stirring, until onion softens. Add wine; bring to a boil. Reduce heat; simmer, uncovered, about 5 minutes or until mixture is reduced by half. Add sauce and stock; bring to a boil.

4 Return meatballs to skillet, reduce heat; simmer, uncovered, about 10 minutes or until meatballs are cooked through. Stir in basil.

5 Cook pasta in pot of boiling salted water, uncovered, until just tender; drain.

6 Divide pasta among bowls; top with meatballs and sauce, serve with cheese.

NUTRITIONAL INFO PER SERVING 45g total fat (13g saturated fat); 11g carbohydrate; 74g protein; 9g fiber; 1193 calories

ricotta gnocchi with fresh tomato sauce

preparation time 10 minutes   **cooking time** 20 minutes   **serves** 4

The Italian word for dumplings, gnocchi can be made with potatoes, flour, ricotta or polenta.

1 pound ricotta cheese
1 cup finely grated parmesan cheese
½ cup all-purpose flour
2 eggs, beaten lightly
1 ½ tablespoons extra virgin olive oil
4 medium tomatoes (about 1 ¾ pounds),
   chopped coarsely
6 green onions, sliced thinly
3 tablespoons coarsely chopped
   fresh oregano
3 tablespoons balsamic vinegar
3 tablespoons extra virgin olive oil,
   for drizzling
½ cup shaved parmesan cheese

1 Bring large pot of salted water to a boil.
2 Combine ricotta, grated parmesan, flour, eggs and oil in large bowl. Drop rounded tablespoons of mixture into boiling water; cook, without stirring, until gnocchi float to the surface. Remove from pot with slotted spoon; drain, cover to keep warm.
3 Combine tomatoes, onions, oregano and vinegar in medium bowl. Top warm gnocchi with fresh tomato sauce; drizzle with olive oil, and top with shaved parmesan.

NUTRITIONAL INFO PER SERVING 41g total fat (18g saturated fat);
19g carbohydrate; 32g protein; 3g fiber; 568 calories

pappardelle with roasted tomato, spinach and feta

preparation time 10 minutes **cooking time** 25 minutes **serves** 4

¼ cup balsamic vinegar

3 cloves garlic, crushed

4 medium tomatoes (about 1 ¼ pounds), cut into eight wedges

12 ounces pappardelle or other wide, long pasta

3 ½ cups baby spinach, trimmed

3 tablespoons olive oil

7 ounces low-fat feta cheese

1 Preheat oven to 400°F.

2 Combine vinegar and garlic in small measuring cup. Place tomatoes, in single layer, on baking sheet; pour vinegar mixture over tomatoes. Roast, uncovered, about 25 minutes or until tomatoes are browned lightly and softened.

3 Cook pasta in large pot of boiling salted water, uncovered, until just tender.

4 Combine drained pasta, tomatoes, spinach and oil in large bowl. Break feta into approximately 1 ¼-inch pieces; add to pasta mixture, toss gently to combine.

NUTRITIONAL INFO PER SERVING 15g total fat (4g saturated fat); 71g carbohydrate; 18g protein; 8g fiber; 492 calories

rotini with crisp salami and tomato sauce

preparation time 15 minutes **cooking time** 15 minutes **serves** 4

1 pound rotini pasta

1 ½ tablespoons olive oil

7 ounces thinly sliced salami,
   cut into strips

2 cloves garlic, crushed

3 small zucchini, sliced thinly

1 teaspoon crushed red pepper flakes

26-ounce jar pasta sauce

1 ¼ cups pitted green olives

1 cup coarsely chopped fresh
   flat-leaf parsley

1 Cook pasta in large pot of boiling salted water, uncovered, until just tender.

2 Heat half of the oil in medium skillet; cook salami, stirring, until crisp. Drain on paper towels.

3 Heat remaining oil in same cleaned skillet; cook garlic and zucchini, stirring, about 2 minutes or until zucchini is just tender. Stir in salami with red pepper flakes, tomato sauce and olives; cook, stirring, until heated through.

4 Place drained pasta and zucchini mixture in large bowl with parsley; toss gently to combine.

NUTRITIONAL INFO PER SERVING 28g total fat (8g saturated fat); 11g carbohydrate; 28g protein; 10g fiber; 834 calories

pad Thai

preparation time 20 minutes **cooking time** 10 minutes **serves** 4

7 ounces dried rice stick noodles

2 cloves garlic, quartered

2 fresh small red serrano or Thai chilies, chopped coarsely

3 tablespoons peanut oil

2 eggs, beaten lightly

1 cup canned fried onions

4-ounce package fried tofu, cut into ¾-inch cubes

¼ cup roasted unsalted peanuts, chopped coarsely

3 cups fresh bean sprouts

6 green onions, sliced thinly

3 tablespoons soy sauce

1 ½ tablespoons fresh lime juice

3 tablespoons coarsely chopped fresh cilantro

1 Place noodles in large heatproof bowl, cover with boiling water; let stand until just tender, drain.

2 Using mortar and pestle, crush garlic and chilies to a paste.

3 Heat 2 teaspoons of the oil in wok. Pour eggs into wok; cook over medium heat, tilting pan, until almost set. Remove omelet from wok; roll tightly, slice thinly.

4 Heat remaining oil in wok, stir-fry garlic paste and fried onions until fragrant. Add tofu; stir-fry 1 minute. Add half the nuts, half the sprouts and half the green onions; stir-fry until spouts are just wilted.

5 Add noodles, soy sauce and lime juice; stir-fry until hot. Remove from heat; sprinkle omelet, cilantro and remaining nuts, sprouts and onions over pad Thai.

NUTRITIONAL INFO PER SERVING 20g total fat (3g saturated fat); 15g carbohydrate; 13g protein; 4g fiber; 298 calories

Singapore noodles

preparation time 15 minutes **cooking time** 10 minutes **serves** 4

1 pound fresh egg noodles

2 teaspoons sesame oil

2 cloves garlic, crushed

¾-inch piece fresh ginger, grated

2 medium carrots, cut into matchsticks

8 ounces cooked small shrimp

1 ½ tablespoons Malaysian curry powder

3 green onions, sliced thinly

1 ½ cups bean sprouts

3 tablespoons soy sauce

¼ cup kecap manis

3 cups (1 pound) shredded
   rotisserie chicken

1 Place noodles in large heatproof bowl; cover with boiling water. Separate noodles with fork; drain.

2 Heat oil in wok; stir-fry garlic, ginger and carrots until carrots are just tender. Add shrimp and curry powder; stir-fry until shrimp change color.

3 Add noodles and remaining ingredients; stir-fry until hot.

Tip You can find kecap manis at Asian markets, or you can make your own by heating equal parts soy sauce and brown sugar, stirring until sugar dissolves.

NUTRITIONAL INFO PER SERVING 16g total fat (5g saturated fat); 33g carbohydrate; 42g protein; 3g fiber; 465 calories

Poultry

The versatility of chicken makes it the perfect choice for a stir fry, a stew, or an elegant main course. In these pages, you'll find classics and inspiring new ideas that are sure to become favorites.

chicken with ham and cheese

preparation time 10 minutes **cooking time** 20 minutes **serves** 4

two 7-ounce boneless, skinless
   chicken breasts
3 tablespoons all-purpose flour
1 egg
1½ tablespoons milk
1 cup dried breadcrumbs
¼ cup vegetable oil
⅓ cup pasta sauce, warmed
4 slices ham (6 ounces)
3 ½ ounces gruyère, emmenthaler or
   Swiss cheese, grated coarsely

1 Preheat broiler.

2 Split chicken breasts in half horizontally. Toss chicken in flour; shake away excess. Dip chicken pieces, one at a time, in combined egg and milk, then in breadcrumbs.

3 Heat oil in large skillet; cook chicken, in batches, until browned and cooked through. Drain on paper towels.

4 Place chicken on baking sheet; divide pasta sauce, ham and cheese on chicken. Place under broiler until cheese melts.

5 Serve with a parmesan and baby arugula salad.

NUTRITIONAL INFO PER SERVING 29g total fat (9g saturated fat); 18g carbohydrate; 43g protein; 1g fiber; 503 calories

prosciutto-wrapped chicken legs with creamy orzo

preparation time 30 minutes **cooking time** 45 minutes **serves** 4

8 stalks fresh rosemary

8 chicken drumsticks (2 ½ pounds)

8 slices prosciutto (4 ounces)

1 cup orzo pasta

1 ½ tablespoons olive oil

1 medium onion, chopped finely

1 clove garlic, crushed

1 ½ cups heavy cream

¼ teaspoon crushed red pepper flakes

8 ounces cherry tomatoes, halved

1 ½ tablespoons fresh thyme

1 pinch grated fresh lemon peel

1 Press one rosemary stalk onto each drumstick; firmly wrap one prosciutto slice around each to hold in place.

2 Cook chicken on heated oiled grill pan until brown all over. Cover chicken; cook about 40 minutes or until cooked to desired degree of doneness.

3 Cook orzo in large pot of boiling salted water until just tender; drain.

4 Heat oil in large skillet; cook onion and garlic, stirring, until onion softens. Add cream and red pepper; simmer, uncovered, until mixture thickens. Add orzo, tomatoes, half the thyme and lemon peel; cook, stirring, until tomatoes just soften. Serve with chicken; sprinkle with remaining thyme.

NUTRITIONAL INFO PER SERVING 60g total fat (29g saturated fat); 43g carbohydrate; 47g protein; 3g fiber; 509 calories

burgers Italian-style

preparation time 20 minutes **cooking time** 30 minutes **serves** 4

1 pound ground chicken

¼ cup drained sun-dried tomatoes, chopped finely

1 ½ tablespoons finely chopped fresh basil

1 egg

1 cup dried breadcrumbs

3 cloves garlic, crushed

4 slices pancetta (2 ounces)

1 square loaf focaccia

½ cup mayonnaise

1 ½ cups baby arugula

4 ounces fresh mozzarella cheese, sliced thickly

1 Combine chicken in large bowl with tomatoes, basil, egg, breadcrumbs and about a third of the garlic; shape mixture into four burgers.

2 Cook burgers on heated oiled grill pan about 30 minutes or until cooked.

3 Cook pancetta on grill pan until crisp. Drain on paper towel.

4 Quarter focaccia; slice each square in half horizontally. Toast cut sides on grill pan.

5 Combine mayonnaise with remaining garlic, spread on focaccia halves; top with arugula, burgers, pancetta and cheese.

NUTRITIONAL INFO PER SERVING 35g total fat (9g saturated fat); 72g carbohydrate; 48g protein; 6g fiber; 803 calories

fried chicken with buttermilk mashed potatoes and gravy

preparation time 15 minutes (plus refrigeration time) **cooking time** 40 minutes **serves** 4

20 chicken drumettes (3 pounds)

1 cup buttermilk

1 cup all-purpose flour

¼ cup Cajun seasoning

½ cup vegetable oil

3 tablespoons butter

5 medium potatoes (about 2 pounds), chopped coarsely

¾ cup buttermilk, warmed

3 tablespoons butter

8 ounces green beans, cut into 1 ½-inch lengths

2 cups chicken stock

1 Combine chicken and 1 cup of buttermilk in large bowl. Cover; refrigerate 3 hours or overnight. Drain; discard buttermilk.

2 Combine flour and seasoning in large bowl; add chicken pieces, toss to coat in mixture. Cover; refrigerate about 30 minutes or until flour forms a paste.

3 Preheat oven to 475°F.

4 Heat oil and butter in large deep skillet; shake excess paste from drumettes back into bowl. Cook chicken, in batches, over medium heat until browned and crisp.

5 Place chicken on wire rack over large baking dish; cook, covered, 15 minutes. Uncover; cook about 10 minutes or until chicken is cooked through and crisp.

6 Boil, steam or microwave potatoes until tender; drain. Mash potatoes in large bowl with ¾ cup of buttermilk and 3 tablespoons of butter until smooth. Cover to keep warm.

7 Boil, steam or microwave beans until tender; drain.

8 To make gravy, add excess paste to skillet; cook, stirring, until mixture bubbles. Gradually stir in stock; cook, stirring, until gravy boils and thickens. Strain gravy into large measuring cup.

9 Serve chicken with mashed potatoes, gravy, and beans.

NUTRITIONAL INFO PER SERVING 70g total fat (23g saturated fat); 64g carbohydrate; 50g protein; 7g fiber; 1097 calories

chicken with herb cheese sauce

preparation time 15 minutes **cooking time** 15 minutes **serves** 4

4 boneless, skinless chicken breasts
(1 ½ pounds)

1 ½ tablespoons olive oil

4 green onions, chopped coarsely

2 teaspoons cornstarch

1 ½ cups chicken stock

3 ½ ounces soft garlic and herb cheese
(such as Boursin)

1 ½ tablespoons coarsely chopped
fresh flat-leaf parsley

1 ½ tablespoons coarsely chopped
fresh chives

1 ½ tablespoons butter

7 ounces green beans, halved

1 clove garlic, crushed

1 medium green bell pepper, sliced thinly

1 medium red bell pepper, sliced thinly

1 Split chicken breasts through center horizontally. Heat oil in large nonstick skillet; cook chicken, in batches, until browned on both sides and cooked through. Remove from skillet; cover to keep warm.

2 Place onions in same skillet; cook, stirring, 2 minutes. Add blended cornstarch and stock; cook, stirring, until mixture boils and thickens. Add cheese; stir until cheese melts. Stir in herbs.

3 Melt butter in medium skillet; cook beans, stirring, until just tender. Add garlic and bell peppers; cook, stirring, until tender.

4 Serve vegetables topped with chicken and sauce.

NUTRITIONAL INFO PER SERVING 26g total fat (11g saturated fat); 6g carbohydrate; 45g protein; 3g fiber; 440 calories

cranberry-glazed chicken wraps

preparation time 15 minutes **cooking time** 20 minutes **serves** 4

¼ cup cranberry sauce

1 ½ tablespoons whole-grain mustard

1 ½ tablespoons lemon juice

2-inch piece fresh ginger, grated

1 clove garlic, crushed

1 pound boneless, skinless
  chicken breasts

1 small red onion, sliced thinly

2 ounces bean sprouts

¼ cup thinly sliced fresh cilantro

¼ cup thinly sliced fresh mint

1 ½ tablespoons white wine vinegar

4 large flour tortillas

1 Heat combined sauce, mustard, lemon juice, ginger and garlic in small pot, stirring, until glaze comes to a boil.

2 Cook chicken, in batches, in large, heated, lightly oiled skillet, brushing frequently with glaze, until cooked through. Cover chicken; let stand 5 minutes before slicing thickly.

3 Place onion, sprouts, herbs and vinegar in medium bowl; toss gently to combine.

4 Heat tortillas on hot griddle or skillet for 1 minute per side or until warm.

5 Divide chicken and salad among centers of tortillas; roll tortillas around filling to form cone shapes.

NUTRITIONAL INFO PER SERVING 6g total fat (1g saturated fat); 31g carbohydrate; 33g protein; 3g fiber; 310 calories

chicken with fontina, pancetta and sage

preparation time 15 minutes **cooking time** 20 minutes **serves** 4

four 7-ounce boneless, skinless
   chicken breasts
4 thin slices fontina cheese
4 slices pancetta (2 ounces)
3 tablespoons coarsely chopped
   fresh sage
3 tablespoons olive oil
2 cloves garlic, crushed
16 whole sage leaves

1 Slit a pocket in one side of each fillet but do not cut all the way through. Divide cheese, pancetta and chopped sage among pockets; secure with toothpicks. Brush chicken with combined oil and garlic.

2 Cook chicken, both sides, on heated oiled grill pan, about 20 minutes or until cooked. Remove toothpicks before serving. Cook whole sage leaves on oiled grill pan until golden brown. Serve chicken topped with sage leaves.

Tip Fontina, a luscious Italian cheese made from cow's milk, has a smooth yet firm texture and a mild, nutty flavor. It is ideal for melting or grilling.

NUTRITIONAL INFO PER SERVING 23g total fat (8g saturated fat); 1g carbohydrate; 55g protein; 1g fiber; 432 calories

chicken stuffed with artichokes and sun-dried tomatoes

preparation time 20 minutes **cooking time** 30 minutes **serves** 4

4 boneless, skinless chicken breasts
   (1 ½ pounds)
8 large fresh basil leaves
8 drained marinated artichoke
   heart quarters
⅔ cup sun-dried tomatoes
5 ounces bocconcini or fresh mozzarella
   cheese, sliced thinly

Arugula and red onion salad
1 ½ tablespoons olive oil
3 tablespoons fresh lemon juice
1 teaspoon Dijon mustard
3 ½ cups baby arugula
½ cup loosely packed fresh basil
1 medium red onion, sliced thinly
1 ½ tablespoons drained baby capers,
   rinsed

1 Using meat mallet, gently pound one chicken breast between sheets of plastic wrap until ½-inch in thickness. Place two of the large basil leaves on one side of chicken breast; top leaves with two artichoke heart quarters, a quarter of the tomatoes and a quarter of the cheese. Fold chicken breast over filling; tie with kitchen string to enclose securely. Repeat process with remaining chicken breasts, basil, artichoke, tomatoes and cheese.

2 Cook chicken, uncovered, on heated oiled grill pan or skillet until browned on both sides. Cover with a heatproof lid or aluminum foil; cook about 15 minutes or until chicken is cooked through.

3 Make arugula and red onion salad.

4 Serve chicken breasts with salad.

Arugula and red onion salad Whisk oil, lemon juice and mustard in large bowl. Add remaining ingredients; toss gently to combine.

NUTRITIONAL INFO PER SERVING 16g total fat (6g saturated fat); 12g carbohydrate; 56g protein; 6g fiber; 427 calories

chicken, lemon and artichoke skewers

preparation time 20 minutes **cooking time** 15 minutes **serves** 4

Soak 12 bamboo skewers in cold water for at least one hour before use to prevent scorching and splintering.

3 tablespoons fresh lemon juice
3 tablespoons olive oil
2 cloves garlic, crushed
2 medium lemons
1 pound boneless, skinless chicken
   breasts, diced into 1 ¼-inch pieces
two 14 ½-ounce cans artichoke hearts,
   drained, halved
24 button mushrooms

1 Whisk together lemon juice, oil and garlic.

2 Cut lemons into 24 pieces. Thread chicken, artichokes, mushrooms and lemons onto 12 skewers. Cook skewers on heated oiled grill pan or grill until chicken is cooked through, brushing skewers with juice mixture while cooking.

NUTRITIONAL INFO PER SERVING 13g total fat (2g saturated fat); 5g carbohydrate; 34g protein; 8g fiber; 280 calories

chicken with pistachio sauce and mashed sweet potatoes

preparation time 15 minutes **cooking time** 20 minutes **serves** 4

2 medium sweet potatoes (1 ¾ pounds),
   chopped coarsely

4 boneless, skinless chicken breasts
   (1 ½ pounds)

2 teaspoons olive oil

1 ½ tablespoons butter

½ cup dry white wine

½ cup chicken stock

⅔ cup heavy cream

3 tablespoons hot water

2 teaspoons fresh thyme

1 pinch grated lemon peel

¼ cup toasted shelled pistachios,
   chopped coarsely

12 ounces green beans

⅓ cup hot milk

1 Boil, steam or microwave sweet potatoes until tender; drain.

2 Slice chicken breasts in half horizontally. Heat oil and half of the butter in large skillet; cook chicken, in batches, until cooked through. Cover to keep warm.

3 Add wine to same skillet; bring to a boil. Stir in stock and cream, reduce heat; simmer, uncovered, about 10 minutes or until sauce thickens slightly. Stir in hot water, thyme, lemon peel and nuts.

4 Boil, steam or microwave beans until tender; drain.

5 Mash sweet potatoes with milk and remaining butter in medium bowl.

6 Serve chicken and sauce with mashed sweet potatoes and beans.

NUTRITIONAL INFO PER SERVING 31g total fat (15g saturated fat); 30g carbohydrate; 47g protein; 6g fiber; 604 calories

chicken, mushroom and fennel pies

preparation time 20 minutes **cooking time** 30 minutes **serves** 4

1 ½ tablespoons olive oil

2 cloves garlic, crushed

1 medium leek, sliced thinly

1 small fennel bulb, sliced thinly

7 ounces button mushrooms, quartered

½ cup dry white wine

4 boneless, skinless chicken breasts
   (1 ¾ pounds), chopped coarsely

1 ½ cups heavy cream

1 ½ tablespoons Dijon mustard

¼ cup coarsely chopped fresh
   flat-leaf parsley

1 sheet puff pastry, cut into quarters

1 egg, beaten lightly

1 ½ tablespoons fennel seeds

1 Preheat oven to 400°F.

2 Heat oil in large pot; cook garlic, leek, fennel and mushrooms, stirring, until vegetables soften.

3 Stir in wine; bring to a boil. Reduce heat; simmer, uncovered, 3 minutes. Add chicken and cream; bring to a boil. Reduce heat; simmer, uncovered, about 10 minutes or until chicken is cooked through and sauce thickens slightly. Stir in mustard and parsley.

4 Place pastry quarters onto baking sheet, brush pastry with egg and sprinkle with seeds; bake about 10 minutes or until golden brown.

5 Divide chicken mixture among serving bowls, top each with pastry.

NUTRITIONAL INFO PER SERVING 53g total fat (29g saturated fat); 21g carbohydrate; 54g protein; 4g fiber; 799 calories

chicken with parmesan polenta and salsa verde

preparation time 10 minutes **cooking time** 20 minutes **serves** 4

1 ½ tablespoons olive oil

4 boneless, skinless chicken breasts
   (1 ½ pounds), halved lengthwise

3 cups chicken stock

1 cup instant polenta

¼ cup finely grated parmesan cheese

⅔ cup milk

2 medium zucchini, quartered lengthwise

Salsa verde

½ cup coarsely chopped fresh
   flat-leaf parsley

¼ cup coarsely chopped fresh basil

1 clove garlic, crushed

2 teaspoons drained baby capers

1 teaspoon Dijon mustard

¼ cup olive oil

2 teaspoons red wine vinegar

1 Heat oil in large skillet; cook chicken, in batches, until browned on both sides and cooked through. Cover to keep warm.

2 Bring stock to a boil in medium pot. Stir in polenta gradually; cook, stirring, until mixture thickens. Add cheese and milk; cook, stirring, until cheese melts.

3 Boil, steam or microwave zucchini until tender; drain.

4 Make salsa verde.

5 Serve chicken on polenta topped with salsa verde.

Salsa verde Combine parsley, basil, garlic and capers in small bowl; whisk in mustard, oil and vinegar until salsa thickens.

NUTRITIONAL INFO PER SERVING 33g total fat (8g saturated fat); 34g carbohydrate; 46g protein; 3g fiber; 618 calories

spiced chicken with fruity couscous

preparation time 5 minutes **cooking time** 20 minutes **serves** 4

4 boneless, skinless chicken breasts
  (1 ½ pounds)
2 teaspoons ground cumin
2 teaspoons ground coriander
3 tablespoons all-purpose flour
3 tablespoons olive oil
½ cup orange juice
1 ½ cups chicken stock
1 teaspoon sugar
1 cup water
4 tablespoons butter, chopped
2 cups couscous
½ cup coarsely chopped dried apricots
¼ cup golden raisins

1 Coat chicken in combined cumin, coriander and flour, shake off excess. Heat oil in large skillet; cook chicken, covered, until browned on both sides and cooked through. Remove from skillet; cover to keep warm.

2 Combine orange juice, a third of the stock and sugar in same skillet; bring to a boil. Reduce heat; simmer, uncovered, about 5 minutes or until mixture thickens slightly.

3 Bring remaining stock and the water to a boil in small pot; add butter, stir until butter melts. Pour liquid over combined couscous and fruit in large heatproof bowl, cover; let stand about 5 minutes or until liquid is absorbed. Fluff with fork. Serve couscous with chicken; drizzle with sauce.

NUTRITIONAL INFO PER SERVING 6g total fat (2g saturated fat); 18g carbohydrate; 10g protein; 1g fiber; 165 calories

chicken kebabs with herb salad

preparation time 20 minutes **cooking time** 15 minutes **serves** 4

Soak 10 bamboo skewers in cold water for at least one hour before use to prevent scorching and splintering.

1 ¾ pounds chicken tenders

2 cloves garlic, crushed

2 teaspoons sweet paprika

3 tablespoons sumac

2 teaspoons finely chopped fresh oregano

3 tablespoons water

1 teaspoon vegetable oil

2 ½ cups coarsely chopped fresh
  flat-leaf parsley

1 cup coarsely chopped fresh cilantro

½ cup coarsely chopped fresh mint

4 medium tomatoes (about 1 ¼ pounds),
  chopped coarsely

1 medium red onion, chopped coarsely

⅓ cup fresh lemon juice

1 ½ tablespoons olive oil

1 Thread chicken onto skewers. Using fingers, rub combined garlic, paprika, sumac, oregano, the water and vegetable oil all over chicken. Cook chicken on heated lightly oiled grill or grill pan until cooked through.

2 Place herbs, tomatoes and onion in medium bowl with lemon juice and olive oil; toss gently to combine.

3 Serve chicken kebabs with herb salad.

Tip Used in Middle-Eastern cooking for centuries, sumac adds its tart, lemony flavor to dips, dressings, barbecued meat, seafood and poultry.

NUTRITIONAL INFO PER SERVING 10g total fat (2g saturated fat); 7g carbohydrate; 38g protein; 5g fiber; 274 calories

Portuguese-style chicken

preparation time 15 minutes (plus refrigeration time) **cooking time** 45 minutes **serves** 4

3 fresh small red serrano or Thai chilies, chopped finely (optional)

2 teaspoons crushed red pepper flakes

3 cloves garlic, crushed

¼ cup cider vinegar

2 teaspoons finely grated lemon peel

⅔ cup fresh lemon juice

2 teaspoons smoked paprika

½ cup finely chopped fresh flat-leaf parsley

2 teaspoons kosher salt

¼ teaspoon cracked black pepper

3 tablespoons olive oil

4 chicken legs and thighs (3 pounds)

1 ½ cups mixed salad greens

1 Combine chilies, red pepper, garlic, vinegar, lemon peel, lemon juice, paprika, parsley, salt, pepper and oil in bowl, add chicken; turn to coat in marinade. Cover; refrigerate 3 hours.

2 Cook chicken, covered, on heated oiled grill or grill pan, over medium heat, about 45 minutes or until cooked through.

3 Serve chicken with salad greens and lemon wedges.

Tip If possible, marinate chicken the night before serving so the flavors can penetrate the chicken.

NUTRITIONAL INFO PER SERVING 42g total fat (12g saturated fat); 2g carbohydrate; 43g protein; 1g fiber; 559 calories

Asian chicken burgers

preparation time 15 minutes **cooking time** 25 minutes **serves** 4

1 teaspoon peanut oil

4-inch stick finely chopped fresh
   lemongrass

1 small red onion, chopped finely

½ teaspoon five-spice powder

½ teaspoon crushed red pepper flakes

1 ½ tablespoons fish sauce

2 teaspoons finely grated lime peel

5-ounce can coconut milk

3 tablespoons crunchy peanut butter

1 pound ground chicken

1 cup stale breadcrumbs

¼ cup finely chopped fresh cilantro

1 egg

2 medium carrots

1 small cucumber

4 hamburger buns

1 Preheat broiler.

2 Heat oil in small skillet; cook lemongrass and onion, stirring, until onion softens. Add five-spice powder, red pepper, fish sauce, lime peel and coconut milk; bring to a boil. Boil sauce mixture, uncovered, until reduced by half; cool 5 minutes.

3 Combine half of the sauce with peanut butter in small bowl. Combine remaining sauce with chicken, breadcrumbs, cilantro and egg in large bowl; use hands to shape chicken mixture into four patties.

4 Using vegetable peeler; slice carrots and cucumber into thin strips.

5 Cook patties in heated, lightly oiled large skillet, uncovered, about 15 minutes or until cooked through.

6 Toast hamburger buns, cut-sides up, under preheated broiler. Spread peanut butter mixture on buns, layer with patties, carrot and cucumber.

NUTRITIONAL INFO PER SERVING 30g total fat (12g saturated fat); 55g carbohydrate; 40g protein; 7g fiber; 657 calories

chicken in lettuce leaf cups

preparation time 10 minutes **cooking time** 15 minutes **serves** 6

4 dried shiitake mushrooms

1 ½ tablespoons peanut oil

2 pounds ground chicken

1 ½-inch piece fresh ginger, chopped finely

1 clove garlic, crushed

8-ounce can water chestnuts, drained,
    chopped coarsely

8-ounce can sliced bamboo shoots,
    drained, chopped coarsely

¼ cup hoisin sauce

¼ cup oyster sauce

3 tablespoons soy sauce

3 tablespoons cornstarch

½ cup chicken stock

3 cups bean sprouts

4 green onions, sliced thickly

18 large Boston lettuce leaves

1 Place mushrooms in small heatproof bowl, cover with boiling water; let stand 20 minutes, drain. Discard stems; chop mushroom caps finely.

2 Heat oil in wok; stir-fry chicken, ginger and garlic until chicken is just changed in color.

3 Add mushrooms, water chestnuts, bamboo shoots, sauces and blended cornstarch and stock; stir-fry until mixture boils and thickens. Stir in sprouts and onions.

4 Divide lettuce leaves among plates; spoon chicken mixture into lettuce leaves.

NUTRITIONAL INFO PER SERVING 18g total fat (5g saturated fat); 15g carbohydrate; 35g protein; 5g fiber; 362 calories

sesame chicken stir fry

preparation time 10 minutes **cooking time** 15 minutes **serves** 4

2 ½ cups jasmine rice

1 ½ tablespoons sesame oil

4 boneless, skinless chicken breasts
   (1 ¾ pounds), sliced thinly

2 cloves garlic, crushed

1 large red bell pepper, sliced thinly

4 tablespoons sweet Thai chili sauce

¼ cup chicken stock

1 pound baby bok choy, halved lengthwise

8-ounce can water chestnuts,
   drained, halved

4 green onions, sliced thinly

1 ½ tablespoons sesame seeds, toasted

1 Cook rice in large pot of boiling water, uncovered, until just tender; drain. Cover to keep warm.

2 Heat half of the oil in wok; stir-fry chicken, in batches, until cooked through. Return chicken to wok with garlic, bell pepper, chili sauce and stock; stir-fry about 2 minutes or until sauce thickens slightly. Remove from wok.

3 Heat remaining oil in same cleaned wok; stir-fry bok choy, chestnuts and onions until bok choy just wilts. Divide bok choy mixture among serving plates; top with chicken, sprinkle with sesame seeds. Serve with rice.

NUTRITIONAL INFO PER SERVING 12g total fat (2g saturated fat); 110g carbohydrate; 57g protein; 6g fiber; 793 calories

Cajun chicken with chunky salsa

preparation time 20 minutes (plus refrigeration time) **cooking time** 20 minutes **serves** 4

4 boneless, skinless chicken breasts
  (1 ½ pounds)

1 teaspoon cracked black pepper

3 tablespoons finely chopped
  fresh oregano

2 teaspoons sweet paprika

1 teaspoon crushed red pepper flakes

2 cloves garlic, crushed

2 teaspoons olive oil

Chunky salsa

2 medium tomatoes, chopped coarsely

1 small red onion, chopped coarsely

1 medium green bell pepper,
  chopped coarsely

3 tablespoons coarsely chopped
  fresh cilantro

2 teaspoons olive oil

3 tablespoons fresh lime juice

1 Place chicken in large bowl with combined remaining ingredients; toss chicken to coat in mixture. Cover; refrigerate 15 minutes.

2 Make chunky salsa.

3 Cook chicken in large, lightly oiled non-stick skillet until cooked through. Serve chicken with salsa.

Chunky salsa Combine ingredients in medium bowl.

NUTRITIONAL INFO PER SERVING 9g total fat (2g saturated fat); 4g carbohydrate; 40g protein; 2g fiber; 259 calories

red curry chicken

preparation time 15 minutes **cooking time** 30 minutes **serves** 4

2 cups jasmine rice

3 tablespoons peanut oil

1 ¾ pounds boneless, skinless chicken
   thighs, chopped coarsely

1 large onion, chopped coarsely

3 cloves garlic, crushed

3 tablespoons red curry paste

1 red serrano or jalapeño pepper,
   halved lengthwise, sliced thinly

1 teaspoon ground cumin

3 baby eggplants, sliced thickly

1 ½ tablespoons fish sauce

3 fresh strips lime peel, sliced thinly

5-ounce can coconut milk

¾ cup water

5 ounces green beans, cut into
   2-inch lengths

⅓ cup loosely packed fresh cilantro

1 Cook rice in large pot of boiling water, uncovered, until just tender; drain.

2 Heat half of the oil in wok; stir-fry chicken, in batches, until browned.

3 Heat remaining oil in same wok; stir-fry onion and garlic until onion softens. Add curry paste, chili and cumin; stir-fry until fragrant. Add eggplants; stir-fry until browned lightly.

4 Return chicken to wok with fish sauce, lime peel, coconut milk, water and beans; stir-fry about 5 minutes or until chicken is cooked through and sauce is thickened slightly.

5 Serve curry and rice sprinkled with cilantro, and lime wedges, if desired.

NUTRITIONAL INFO PER SERVING 34g total fat (13g saturated fat); 87g carbohydrate; 46g protein; 6g fiber; 851 calories

Thai lime chicken with bok choy

preparation time 10 minutes **cooking time** 15 minutes **serves** 4

1 ½ tablespoons peanut oil

8 boneless, skinless chicken thighs
  (about 2 pounds)

1 ½ tablespoons fish sauce

3 tablespoons fresh lime juice

3 tablespoons brown sugar

1 clove garlic, crushed

1 fresh small red serrano or Thai chili,
  chopped finely

10 ½ ounces baby bok choy,
  quartered lengthwise

1 lime, cut into four slices

2 green onions, sliced thinly

¼ cup firmly packed fresh cilantro

1 Heat oil in large skillet; cook chicken, in batches, until cooked through.

2 Whisk together fish sauce, lime juice, sugar, garlic and chili.

3 Boil, steam or microwave bok choy until tender; drain.

4 Add lime slices to same large skillet; cook until browned on both sides.

5 Divide chicken among serving plates; spoon dressing over chicken, top with onions and cilantro. Serve with bok choy, lime slices and steamed jasmine rice, if desired.

NUTRITIONAL INFO PER SERVING 21g total fat (6g saturated fat); 8g carbohydrate; 43g protein; 2g fiber; 388 calories

chicken and mushroom stir fry with crispy noodles

preparation time 15 minutes **cooking time** 20 minutes **serves** 4

1 ½ tablespoons peanut oil

2 pounds boneless, skinless chicken
   thighs, sliced thinly

2 cloves garlic, crushed

8 green onions, chopped coarsely

7 ounces shiitake mushrooms,
   chopped coarsely

7 ounces Chinese broccoli or bok choy,
   chopped coarsely

3 ½ ounces oyster mushrooms,
   chopped coarsely

⅓ cup oyster sauce

3 ½ ounces enoki mushrooms

2 ounces fried chow mein noodles

1 Heat oil in wok; stir-fry chicken, in batches, until cooked.

2 Return chicken to wok with garlic and onions; stir-fry until onions soften.
Add shiitake mushrooms; stir-fry until tender. Add Chinese broccoli or bok choy,
oyster mushrooms and sauce; stir-fry until vegetables are tender.

3 Remove from heat; toss in enoki mushrooms and noodles.

NUTRITIONAL INFO PER SERVING 24g total fat (7g saturated fat);
16g carbohydrate; 51g protein; 5g fiber; 494 calories

sweet and spicy chicken with noodles

preparation time 20 minutes (plus refrigeration time) **cooking time** 20 minutes **serves** 4

¼ cup sweet Thai chili sauce

3 tablespoons plum sauce

1¾ pounds boneless, skinless chicken
thighs, sliced thinly

1 pound pre-cooked stir-fry (hokkien)
noodles

8-ounce can water chestnuts, drained,
rinsed, halved

8 green onions, sliced thickly

1 Thai chili, sliced thinly

2 cloves garlic, crushed

10 ½ ounces bok choy, trimmed,
chopped coarsely

1 Combine sauces with chicken in large bowl. Cover; refrigerate 1 hour.

2 Heat oiled wok; stir-fry chicken mixture, in batches, until browned.

3 Place noodles in medium heatproof bowl; cover with boiling water, separate with fork, drain.

4 Stir-fry chestnuts, onions, chili and garlic in wok for 2 minutes. Return chicken to wok with bok choy; stir-fry until chicken is cooked. Serve with noodles.

NUTRITIONAL INFO PER SERVING 15g total fat (4g saturated fat); 43g carbohydrate; 41g protein; 5g fiber; 481 calories

hoisin chicken stir fry

preparation time 15 minutes (plus refrigeration time) **cooking time** 15 minutes **serves** 4

1 ¾ pounds boneless, skinless chicken
   breasts, sliced thinly
2 cloves garlic, crushed
1 ½ teaspoons five-spice powder
4-inch stick fresh lemongrass,
   chopped finely
¾-inch piece fresh ginger, grated
3 tablespoons peanut oil
1 medium onion, sliced thinly
1 serrano pepper, chopped finely
1 medium red bell pepper, sliced thickly
⅓ cup hoisin sauce
2 teaspoons finely grated lemon peel
1 ½ tablespoons lemon juice
½ cup coarsely chopped fresh cilantro
3 tablespoons canned fried onions
1 green onion, sliced thinly

1 Combine chicken with half the garlic, 1 teaspoon of the five-spice and all of
the lemongrass and ginger in large bowl. Cover, refrigerate.
2 Heat half the oil in wok; stir-fry onion, serrano pepper, bell pepper and remaining
garlic until onion softens. Remove from wok.
3 Heat remaining oil in wok; stir-fry chicken, in batches, until cooked.
4 Return onion mixture and chicken to wok with hoisin sauce, lemon peel, lemon
juice and remaining five-spice powder; stir-fry until sauce thickens slightly. Remove
from heat; toss cilantro into stir-fry, sprinkle with shallots and green onion.

Tip If possible, marinate the chicken the night before serving so the flavors can
penetrate the chicken.

NUTRITIONAL INFO PER SERVING 15g total fat (3g saturated fat);
12g carbohydrate; 47g protein; 4g fiber; 383 calories

barley risotto with chicken and tarragon

preparation time 15 minutes **cooking time** 40 minutes **serves** 4

Pearl barley is barley that has had the husk removed, then been hulled and polished, much the same as rice.

1½ tablespoons olive oil

1 pound boneless, skinless chicken
  breasts, sliced thinly

3 cups chicken stock

2 cups water

1 medium onion, chopped finely

1 clove garlic, crushed

2 medium leeks (about 1½ pounds),
  sliced thinly

¾ cup pearl barley

⅓ cup dry white wine

1 cup frozen peas

3 tablespoons finely chopped
  fresh tarragon

1 Heat half of the oil in large pot; cook chicken, in batches, until browned lightly and cooked through. Cover to keep warm.

2 Combine stock and water in large pot; bring to a boil. Reduce heat; simmer, covered.

3 Heat remaining oil in cleaned pot; cook onion, garlic and leeks, stirring, until onion softens. Add barley; stir to combine with onion mixture. Add wine; cook, stirring, until almost evaporated. Stir in ½ cup of the simmering stock mixture; cook, stirring, over low heat until liquid is absorbed. Continue adding stock mixture, ½ cup at a time, stirring until absorbed after each addition. Total cooking time should be about 30 minutes or until barley is just tender.

4 Add chicken and peas to risotto; cook, stirring, until peas are just tender. Remove from heat; stir in tarragon.

NUTRITIONAL INFO PER SERVING 10g total fat (2g saturated fat); 32g carbohydrate; 38g protein; 10g fiber; 379 calories

chicken with honey mustard sauce

preparation time 15 minutes **cooking time** 20 minutes **serves** 4

2 tablespoons olive oil

four ½-pound chicken breast fillets

3 shallots, finely chopped

1 clove garlic, crushed

½ cup dry white wine

½ cup chicken stock

2 tablespoons honey

2 teaspoons Dijon mustard

½ cup roasted pecans, chopped coarsely

1 tablespoon lemon juice

4 ounces mixed salad greens

2 small pears (about ¾ pound),
   sliced thinly

1 Heat half of oil in large skillet; sauté chicken, uncovered, until cooked through. Remove from skillet, cover to keep warm.

2 Add shallots and garlic to same skillet, stirring until shallots soften. Add wine; bring to a boil. Reduce heat; simmer, uncovered, until reduced by half. Add chicken stock, honey and mustard; cook, stirring, about 5 minutes or until reduced by half. Remove from heat; stir in pecans.

3 Combine lemon juice and remaining oil in medium bowl, add greens; toss gently to combine.

4 Cut chicken in half crosswise; drizzle with sauce. Serve chicken with dressed mesclun and pears.

NUTRITIONAL INFO PER SERVING 7g total fat (1g saturated fat); 5g carbohydrate; 11g protein; 1g fiber; 134 calories

almond and cilantro crusted chicken with lemon mayonnaise

preparation time 15 minutes **cooking time** 10 minutes **serves** 4

1 ½ cups almond meal

2 teaspoons crushed red pepper flakes

½ cup finely chopped fresh cilantro leaves

1 tablespoon grated lemon peel

2 eggs

four ½-pound chicken breast fillets

⅓ cup all-purpose flour

vegetable oil, for shallow-frying

Lemon mayonnaise

⅔ cup mayonnaise

1 teaspoon grated lemon peel

¼ cup fresh lemon juice

1 Preheat oven to 400°F.

2 Make lemon mayonnaise.

3 Combine almond meal, crushed red pepper, cilantro and lemon peel in shallow medium bowl. Whisk eggs lightly in another shallow medium bowl. Coat chicken in flour mixture; shake off excess. Dip chicken in egg, and coat in almond mixture again. Repeat with remaining chicken breasts.

4 Heat oil in large skillet; cook chicken, in batches, until browned. Place chicken on large baking sheet; bake, uncovered, about 10 minutes or until cooked through. Slice chicken into thick pieces; serve with mayonnaise.

Lemon mayonnaise Combine ingredients in small bowl.

Tip Make your own almond meal by grinding whole almonds in a food processor until it resembles a fine powder.

NUTRITIONAL INFO PER SERVING 82g total fat (11g saturated fat); 22g carbohydrate; 57g protein; 5g fiber; 1053 calories

chicken with horseradish cream and sautéed spinach

preparation time 10 minutes **cooking time** 20 minutes **serves** 4

1 tablespoon olive oil

four ½-pound boneless, skinless
chicken breast

1 green onion, sliced thinly

2 tablespoons dry white wine

⅔ cup heavy cream

2 tablespoons prepared horseradish

2 teaspoons fresh lemon juice

½ teaspoon dijon mustard

1 teaspoon finely chopped fresh dill

1 tablespoon butter

2 cloves garlic, crushed

10 ounces fresh spinach,
chopped coarsely

1 Heat 1 ½ teaspoons of the oil in large skillet; cook chicken until cooked through. Remove from skillet; cover, and keep warm.

2 Add remaining oil to same skillet. Cook onion, stirring, until soft. Add wine; bring to a boil. Reduce heat; simmer, uncovered, until reduced by half. Add cream; bring to a boil. Reduce heat; simmer, uncovered, about 2 minutes or until sauce thickens slightly. Add horseradish, lemon juice, mustard and dill; stir until heated through.

3 Melt butter in large pot. Add garlic; cook, stirring, 2 minutes. Add spinach; cook over low heat, covered, about 2 minutes or until wilted.

4 Serve chicken and spinach drizzled with sauce. Top with a sprig of fresh dill.

Tip Be sure to use prepared white horseradish, not cream-style horseradish for this recipe.

NUTRITIONAL INFO PER SERVING 39g total fat (19g saturated fat); 4g carbohydrate; 48g protein; 5g fiber; 566 calories

chicken alla pizzaiola

preparation time 20 minutes   **cooking time** 40 minutes   **serves** 4

⅓ cup olive oil

2 cloves garlic, crushed

½ cup dry white wine

½ cup chicken stock

two 14 ½-ounce cans crushed tomatoes,
   undrained

3 tablespoons coarsely chopped
   fresh oregano

3 tablespoons coarsely chopped
   fresh flat-leaf parsley

½ cup pitted Kalamata olives

4 boneless, skinless chicken thighs
   (1 pound)

¼ cup all-purpose flour

2 eggs

1 ½ tablespoons milk

1 cup dried breadcrumbs

7 slices prosciutto (4 ounces)

1 ¾ cups grated mozzarella cheese

8 ounces fettucine

1 Preheat oven to 400°F.

2 Heat half of the oil in medium skillet; cook garlic, stirring, over low heat, until fragrant. Add wine and stock; bring to a boil. Reduce heat; simmer, uncovered, 3 minutes. Add undrained tomatoes, oregano and parsley; bring to a boil. Reduce heat; simmer, uncovered, about 10 minutes or until pizzaiola sauce thickens slightly. Stir in olives.

3 Toss chicken in flour; shake away excess. Dip chicken thighs, one at a time, in combined eggs and milk, then breadcrumbs. Heat remaining oil in large skillet; cook chicken, in batches, until browned lightly.

4 Place chicken, in single layer, in medium shallow baking dish; top with prosciutto, then pizzaiola sauce, then cheese. Bake, uncovered, about 20 minutes or until chicken is cooked through.

5 Cook pasta in large pot of boiling water, uncovered, until just tender; drain. Serve pasta topped with chicken pizzaiola.

NUTRITIONAL INFO PER SERVING 42g total fat (13g saturated fat); 72g carbohydrate; 53g protein; 6g fiber; 914 calories

chermoulla chicken with chickpea salad

preparation time 25 minutes   **cooking time** 20 minutes   **serves** 4

14 ½-ounce can chickpeas, rinsed
   and drained
4 boneless, skinless chicken breasts
   (1 ½ pounds)
1 medium red bell pepper, chopped finely
1 medium green bell pepper,
   chopped finely
2 large plum tomatoes, chopped finely
1 small white onion, chopped finely
3 tablespoons fresh lemon juice

Chermoulla
½ cup finely chopped fresh cilantro
½ cup finely chopped fresh flat-leaf parsley
3 cloves garlic, crushed
3 tablespoons white wine vinegar
3 tablespoons fresh lemon juice
1 teaspoon sweet paprika
½ teaspoon ground cumin
3 tablespoons olive oil

1 Combine ingredients for chermoulla in large bowl; reserve half of the chermoulla for chickpea salad.

2 Place chicken in bowl with remaining half of the chermoulla; turn chicken to coat in chermoulla. Cook chicken, in batches, on heated oiled grill or grill pan until cooked through. Cover to keep warm.

3 Place chickpeas in large bowl with bell peppers, tomatoes, onion and remaining chermoulla; toss gently to combine. Serve chickpea salad with sliced chicken, drizzled with juice.

NUTRITIONAL INFO PER SERVING 22g total fat (5g saturated fat); 23g carbohydrate; 47g protein; 9g fiber; 477 calories

turkey cutlets with mustard cream sauce and bacon mashed potatoes

preparation time 15 minutes **cooking time** 30 minutes **serves** 4

1 ½ tablespoons butter

8 turkey cutlets (2 pounds)

2 shallots, chopped finely

1 clove garlic, crushed

½ cup dry white wine

½ cup heavy cream

2 teaspoons whole-grain mustard

Bacon mashed potatoes

2 pounds medium potatoes,
  chopped coarsely

3-4 slices bacon (5 ounces),
  chopped coarsely

1 ½ tablespoons butter

¼ cup heavy cream

1 ½ tablespoons coarsely chopped
  fresh chives

1 Make bacon mashed potatoes.

2 Melt half of the butter in large skillet; cook cutlets, in batches, until browned on both sides.

3 Melt remaining butter in same skillet; cook shallots and garlic, stirring, until soft. Add wine; bring to a boil. Reduce heat; simmer, uncovered, about 5 minutes or until almost evaporated. Stir in cream and mustard. Return cutlets to skillet; bring to a boil. Reduce heat; simmer, covered, about 10 minutes or until turkey is cooked through.

4 Serve cutlets with bacon mashed potatoes, drizzled with sauce.

Bacon mashed potatoes Boil, steam or microwave potatoes until tender; drain. Cook bacon in small skillet; drain on paper towels. Mash potatoes in large bowl with butter and cream until smooth. Stir in bacon and chives.

NUTRITIONAL INFO PER SERVING 37g total fat (21g saturated fat); 31g carbohydrate; 52g protein; 4g fiber; 698 calories

duck breasts with fig sauce and spinach orzo

preparation time 20 minutes **cooking time** 25 minutes **serves** 4

4 duck breast fillets (1 ¼ pounds)

4 sprigs fresh rosemary

4 bay leaves

7 ounces dried orzo

1 ½ tablespoons butter

7 cups baby spinach

1 small onion, chopped finely

6 dried figs, quartered

1 cup port

1 cup chicken stock

1 ½ tablespoons butter

1 Use fingers to make a pocket between meat and fat of each duck breast; press 1 sprig rosemary and 1 bay leaf into each pocket. Prick duck skins with fork several times; cook duck, skin-side down, in large, heated lightly oiled skillet about 8 minutes or until browned and crisp. Turn duck; cook about 5 minutes or until cooked as desired. Remove from skillet; cover to keep warm.

2 Cook pasta in large pot of boiling salted water, uncovered, until just tender; drain. Place pasta in large bowl with butter and spinach; toss gently to combine. Cover to keep warm.

3 Cook onion in same skillet as duck, stirring, until soft. Add figs, port and stock; bring to a boil. Reduce heat; simmer, stirring, about 5 minutes or until sauce thickens. Add 1 ½ tablespoons of butter; whisk until sauce is combined.

4 Slice duck thinly; serve with orzo and fig sauce.

NUTRITIONAL INFO PER SERVING 18g total fat (8g saturated fat); 6g carbohydrate; 36g protein; 7g fiber; 600 calories

duck breasts with five-spice and honey peaches

preparation time 10 minutes **cooking time** 20 minutes **serves** 4

¼ cup honey

1 teaspoon five-spice powder

4 medium peaches (about 1 ¼ pounds), quartered

4 boneless, skinless duck breasts (1 ¼ pounds)

1 ½ tablespoons red wine vinegar

3 tablespoons olive oil

1 teaspoon Dijon mustard

1 shallot, chopped finely

3 ½ ounces snow peas, trimmed, halved

3 ½ cups baby spinach leaves

1 Cook honey, five-spice and peaches in large heated skillet, stirring, about 5 minutes or until peaches are browned lightly. Remove from skillet; cover to keep warm.

2 Score duck skins; cook duck, skin-side down, in same skillet, over medium heat, about 10 minutes or until browned and crisp. Turn duck; cook about 5 minutes or until cooked to desired degree of doneness. Remove from skillet; cover to keep warm.

3 Combine vinegar, oil, mustard and shallot in large bowl. Add snow peas and spinach; toss gently to combine.

4 Slice duck thinly; serve with peaches and salad.

NUTRITIONAL INFO PER SERVING 18g total fat (4g saturated fat); 28g carbohydrate; 29g protein; 3g fiber; 393 calories

Seafood

One of the most appealing ways to eat healthfully is to eat fish. These recipes rely on fresh ingredients, simple techniques — and deliver big flavor.

salmon in sesame crust

preparation time 10 minutes **cooking time** 10 minutes **serves** 4

2 cups medium-grain white rice

3 tablespoons sesame seeds

1 teaspoon coriander seeds

1 teaspoon black peppercorns

four 7½-ounce skinless salmon fillets

1½ tablespoons vegetable oil

1½ tablespoons sesame oil

1 clove garlic, crushed

1 teaspoon grated fresh ginger

1 small red serrano or Thai chili, seeded, sliced thinly lengthwise (optional)

1 pound baby bok choy, quartered lengthwise

¼ cup low-sodium soy sauce

1½ tablespoons mirin or white wine

3 tablespoons honey

3 tablespoons fresh lime juice

1 Cook rice in large pot of boiling water, uncovered, until just tender; drain. Cover to keep warm.

2 Place seeds and peppercorns in strong plastic bag; crush with rolling pin or meat mallet. Coat one side of each fish fillet with sesame mixture.

3 Heat vegetable oil in large skillet; cook fish, sesame-side down, uncovered, for 1 minute. Turn fish; cook, uncovered, until desired degree of doneness.

4 Heat sesame oil in skillet; stir-fry garlic, ginger and chili until fragrant. Add remaining ingredients; stir-fry until bok choy just wilts.

5 Serve fish with rice and bok choy.

NUTRITIONAL INFO PER SERVING 27g total fat (5g saturated fat); 93g carbohydrate; 49g protein; 3g fiber; 827 calories

spicy grilled shrimp with fresh mango salsa

preparation time 25 minutes **cooking time** 10 minutes **serves** 4

2 pounds uncooked large shrimp

½ teaspoon ground turmeric

1 teaspoon chili powder

2 teaspoons sweet paprika

2 cloves garlic, crushed

Mango salsa

2 large mangoes (about 2 ½ pounds),
  chopped coarsely

1 small red onion, sliced thinly

1 fresh serrano pepper, seeded,
  sliced thinly

1 ½ cups bean sprouts

½ cup coarsely chopped fresh cilantro

2 teaspoons fish sauce

2 teaspoons brown sugar

3 tablespoons fresh lime juice

1 ½ tablespoons peanut oil

1 Make mango salsa.

2 Peel and devein shrimp, leaving tails intact. Combine turmeric, serrano pepper, paprika and garlic in large bowl, add shrimp; toss shrimp to coat in mixture.

3 Cook shrimp, in batches, on heated oiled grill or grill pan until browned lightly. Serve shrimp with salad.

Mango salsa Place ingredients in medium bowl; toss gently to combine.

NUTRITIONAL INFO PER SERVING 6g total fat (1g saturated fat); 30g carbohydrate; 30g protein; 5g fiber; 294 calories

lobster tails with lime butter and pineapple mint salsa

preparation time 20 minutes **cooking time** 10 minutes **serves** 4

7 tablespoons butter

1 teaspoon finely grated lime peel

1 fresh small red serrano or jalapeño
  pepper, chopped finely (optional)

¾-inch piece fresh ginger, grated

4 uncooked small lobster tails in shells
  (1 ¼ pounds)

Pineapple mint salsa

1 small pineapple (2 pounds),
  chopped coarsely

3 tablespoons fresh lime juice

½ cup finely chopped fresh mint

1 fresh small red serrano or jalapeño
  pepper, chopped finely

1 Make pineapple mint salsa.

2 Melt butter in small pot; cook lime peel, pepper and ginger, stirring, 2 minutes.

3 Using scissors, cut soft shell from underneath lobster tails to expose meat;
cut lobster tails in half lengthwise. Brush with butter mixture; cook, in batches,
on heated oiled grill pan until cooked through. Serve with salsa.

Pineapple mint salsa Combine ingredients in medium bowl.

NUTRITIONAL INFO PER SERVING 22g total fat (14g saturated fat);
10g carbohydrate; 31g protein; 3g fiber; 368 calories

salt and Szechwan pepper salmon with wasabi mayonnaise

preparation time 10 minutes **cooking time** 15 minutes **serves** 4

Szechwan peppercorns aren't really peppercorns — they are fragrant, slightly woody berries with an intense, citrus-like flavor.

2 teaspoons sea salt or kosher salt
2 teaspoons Szechwan peppercorns
¼ cup vegetable oil
four ½-pound salmon fillets, skin on
½ cup mayonnaise
2 teaspoons wasabi paste
1 teaspoon finely chopped fresh cilantro
1 teaspoon fresh lime juice

1 Using mortar and pestle or pepper grinder, grind salt and peppercorns until fine. Combine peppercorn mixture, 2 tablespoons of the oil and salmon in large bowl, cover; let stand 5 minutes.

2 Combine mayonnaise, wasabi, cilantro and lime juice in small bowl.

3 Heat remaining oil in large skillet; cook fish, skin-side down, until skin crisps. Turn fish; cook, uncovered, until cooked to desired degree of doneness.

4 Serve fish with wasabi mayonnaise and lime wedges.

NUTRITIONAL INFO PER SERVING 40g total fat (6g saturated fat); 8g carbohydrate; 39g protein; 1g fiber; 545 calories

pancetta wrapped fish with herb-caper butter

preparation time 15 minutes **cooking time** 10 minutes **serves** 4

We used snapper fillets for this recipe, but any firm white fish fillet can be used.

6 tablespoons butter, softened

3 tablespoons coarsely chopped
   fresh flat-leaf parsley

1 ½ tablespoons drained capers, rinsed

2 cloves garlic, quartered

2 green onions, chopped coarsely

8 slices pancetta (4 ounces)

4 white fish fillets (1 ¼ pounds)

1 ½ tablespoons olive oil

12 ounces asparagus, trimmed

1 Blend or process butter, parsley, capers, garlic and onions until mixture forms a smooth paste.

2 Spread 2 tablespoons of the butter mixture and two slices of the pancetta on each fish fillet.

3 Heat oil in large heavy skillet; cook fish, pancetta-side down, until pancetta is crisp. Turn fish carefully; cook, uncovered, until desired degree of doneness.

4 Boil, steam or microwave asparagus until tender.

5 Serve fish and asparagus drizzled with pan juices.

NUTRITIONAL INFO PER SERVING 25g total fat (14g saturated fat); 2g carbohydrate; 38g protein; 1g fiber; 417 calories

cod with grilled corn salad

preparation time 15 minutes **cooking time** 20 minutes **serves** 4

four 7-ounce cod fillets
3 tablespoons soy sauce

Grilled corn salad
2 ears fresh corn (1 pound), silk and
   husks removed
8 ounces cherry tomatoes, halved
1 small red onion, sliced thinly
1 fresh jalapeño pepper, seeded,
   sliced thinly
2 medium avocados (1 pound),
   chopped coarsely
¼ cup coarsely chopped fresh cilantro
⅓ cup fresh lime juice
1 clove garlic, crushed
1½ tablespoons olive oil

1 Make grilled corn salad.
2 Brush fish with soy sauce; cook on heated lightly oiled grill or grill pan until browned on both sides until desired degree of doneness. Serve fish with salad.
Grilled corn salad Cook corn on heated oiled grill or grill pan until browned and just tender; cool 10 minutes. Using sharp knife, remove kernels from cob; combine in medium bowl with remaining ingredients.

NUTRITIONAL INFO PER SERVING 30g total fat (6g saturated fat);
19g carbohydrate; 48g protein; 7g fiber; 584 calories

quick-and-easy shrimp and pea risotto

preparation time 5 minutes **cooking time** 25 minutes **serves** 4

1 ¼ pounds cooked large shrimp

1 ½ tablespoons butter

1 small leek, sliced thinly

2 cloves garlic, crushed

8 saffron threads

2 cups arborio rice

2 cups boiling water

1 cup dry white wine

1 ½ cups fish stock

1 cup frozen peas

3 tablespoons coarsely chopped
  fresh chives

¼ cup fresh lemon juice

2 tablespoons butter

1 Peel and devein shrimp, leaving tails intact.

2 Place 1 ½ tablespoons butter, leek, garlic and saffron in large microwave-safe bowl; cook in microwave oven on high (100%), covered, about 2 minutes or until leek softens. Stir in rice; cook on high (100%), covered, 1 minute. Add the water, wine and stock; cook on high (100%), covered, 15 minutes, pausing to stir three times during cooking.

3 Add peas and shrimp (reserve a few for garnish, if desired); cook on high (100%), covered, 3 minutes. Stir in chives, lemon juice and 2 tablespoons butter.

NUTRITIONAL INFO PER SERVING 12g total fat (7g saturated fat); 85g carbohydrate; 26g protein; 4g fiber; 604 calories

snapper with red pepper remoulade and fried potatoes

preparation time 25 minutes **cooking time** 30 minutes **serves** 4

3 large potatoes (2 pounds), unpeeled,
   cut into ½-inch slices

¼ cup olive oil

1 ½ tablespoons canned fried onions

½ teaspoon crushed red pepper flakes

2 teaspoons sea salt or kosher salt

four 9-ounce snapper fillets

¼ cup all-purpose flour

Red pepper remoulade

⅓ cup roasted red bell peppers,
   drained, sliced thinly

⅓ cup mayonnaise

1 ½ tablespoons drained capers, rinsed,
   chopped finely

2 drained anchovy fillets, chopped finely

1 ½ tablespoons finely chopped fresh
   flat-leaf parsley

2 teaspoons fresh lemon juice

1 Boil, steam or microwave potatoes until tender; drain. Combine in medium bowl with oil.

2 Crush onions, red pepper flakes and salt finely using mortar and pestle.

3 Make red pepper remoulade.

4 Coat fish in flour; shake off excess.

5 Cook potato slices, in batches, in heated oiled flat skillet until browned on both sides. Sprinkle with salt-onion mixture; cover to keep warm.

6 Cook fish in heated oiled skillet until browned on both sides and cooked through.

7 Serve fish with remoulade and potatoes.

Red pepper remoulade Combine all ingredients in small bowl.

NUTRITIONAL INFO PER SERVING 28g total fat (5g saturated fat); 42g carbohydrate; 63g protein; 4g fiber; 689 calories

tilapia with chunky tomato caper sauce

preparation time 15 minutes **cooking time** 15 minutes **serves** 4

1 tablespoon olive oil

four ½-pound tilapia fillets

1 medium yellow onion, chopped finely

2 cloves garlic, crushed

4 medium tomatoes, peeled, seeded,
   chopped coarsely

4 drained anchovy fillets, chopped finely

1 tablespoon drained capers, rinsed

1 teaspoon sugar

¼ cup coarsely chopped fresh
   flat-leaf parsley

1 Heat 1 ½ teaspoons of the oil in large skillet; cook fish, uncovered, until cooked to desired degree of doneness.

2 Heat remaining oil in small pot; cook onion and garlic, stirring, until onion softens. Add tomato; cook, stirring, 1 minute. Remove from heat; stir in anchovies, capers, sugar and parsley. Top fish with sauce. Serve with lemon wedges.

NUTRITIONAL INFO PER SERVING 7g total fat (1g saturated fat); 6g carbohydrate; 42g protein; 3g fiber; 263 calories

shrimp and swordfish skewers with coconut rice

preparation time 25 minutes **cooking time** 25 minutes **serves** 4

You'll need to soak eight bamboo skewers in cold water for at least an hour before use to prevent them splintering and scorching.

four 10-ounce swordfish fillets
16 fresh large shrimp (2 ½ pounds),
peeled and deveined with tails intact
1 tablespoon ground cumin
2 teaspoons ground coriander
½ teaspoon chili powder
¼ cup peanut oil
2 teaspoons fish sauce
2 teaspoons fresh lime juice

Coconut rice
1 ¾ cups white long-grain rice
1 ⅔ cups canned coconut milk
2 ¼ cups water
⅓ cup flaked coconut
¾ cup loosely packed fresh cilantro leaves

1 Make coconut rice.
2 Cut each fillet into six pieces. Thread alternate pieces of fish and shrimp on skewers.
3 Combine spices, oil, fish sauce, and lime juice in small bowl; brush over fish and shrimp. Cook skewers on grill pan (or grill) until browned on all sides and cooked to desired degree of doneness. Serve skewers with coconut rice.

Coconut rice Combine rice, coconut milk, and 2 ¼ cups water in large, heavy pot; bring to a boil, stirring occasionally. Reduce heat; simmer, covered, about 20 minutes or until liquid is absorbed and rice is just tender. Heat dry small skillet; cook flaked coconut, stirring over low heat until lightly browned. Stir toasted coconut and cilantro into rice.

NUTRITIONAL INFO PER SERVING 45g total fat (25g saturated fat); 73g carbohydrate; 98g protein; 4g fiber; 1102 calories

grilled shrimp with tropical fruits

preparation time 15 minutes **cooking time** 15 minutes **serves** 4

24 uncooked jumbo shrimp (3½ pounds)

¼ medium pineapple, chopped coarsely

1 slightly firm large mango (about
   1 ¼ pounds), chopped coarsely

1 slightly firm large banana,
   chopped coarsely

¼ cup loosely packed fresh mint

3 tablespoons fresh lime juice

Dressing

½ cup loosely packed fresh mint

½ cup loosely packed fresh
   flat-leaf parsley

1 clove garlic, quartered

3 tablespoons lime juice

1 ½ tablespoons olive oil

1 Make dressing.

2 Cook shrimp on heated lightly oiled grill pan or skillet until changed in color and cooked through.

3 Cook fruit on same grill pan until browned lightly.

4 Combine shrimp and fruit in large bowl with mint and lime juice. Divide shrimp mixture among serving bowls; drizzle with dressing.

Dressing Blend or process ingredients until combined.

NUTRITIONAL INFO PER SERVING 6g total fat (1g saturated fat); 25g carbohydrate; 44g protein; 5g fiber; 335 calories

Thai fish burger

preparation time 20 minutes **cooking time** 15 minutes **serves** 4

You can find kecap manis at Asian markets, or you can make your own by heating equal parts soy sauce and molasses or brown sugar, stirring until molasses or sugar dissolves.

1 pound cod (or other firm white fish) fillets, chopped coarsely

1 ½ tablespoons fish sauce

1 ½ tablespoons kecap manis

1 clove garlic, quartered

1 fresh small red serrano or Thai chili, chopped coarsely

2 ounces green beans, trimmed, chopped coarsely

¼ cup canned fried onions

¼ cup coarsely chopped fresh cilantro

2 cups baby spinach

1 cucumber, seeded, sliced thinly

1 ½ tablespoons fresh lime juice

2 teaspoons brown sugar

2 teaspoons fish sauce

4 hamburger buns

⅓ cup sweet Thai chili sauce (optional)

1 Blend or process fish, 1 ½ tablespoons fish sauce, kecap manis, garlic and chili until smooth. Combine fish mixture in large bowl with beans, fried onions and cilantro; shape into four patties.

2 Cook patties on heated oiled flat plate about 15 minutes or until cooked.

3 Combine spinach, cucumber, lime juice, sugar and 2 teaspoons fish sauce in medium bowl.

4 Toast buns, top with spinach salad, chili sauce, and burgers.

NUTRITIONAL INFO PER SERVING 5g total fat (1g saturated fat); 55g carbohydrate; 32g protein; 6g fiber; 412 calories

seared tuna with wasabi soba noodles

preparation time 20 minutes **cooking time** 15 minutes **serves** 4

Wasabi is Japanese horseradish sold in powdered or paste form. Soba are Japanese buckwheat noodles and are great served hot or cold.

four 7-ounce tuna steaks
3 tablespoons mirin or dry white wine
1 ½ tablespoons tamarind puree
14 ounces soba noodles
3 tablespoons toasted sesame seeds
4 green onions, sliced thinly lengthwise
¼ cup soy sauce
1 teaspoon wasabi paste
2 teaspoons sesame oil
3 tablespoons lime juice

1 Place fish in medium bowl with combined mirin and tamarind; toss to coat fish in mirin mixture.

2 Cook soba in large pot of boiling water, uncovered, until just tender; drain. Rinse under cold water; drain.

3 Cook fish, in batches, on heated oiled grill pan or skillet until browned on both sides and cooked to desired degree of doneness.

4 Combine noodles in medium bowl with sesame seeds and all but 1 ½ tablespoons of the onions. Whisk together soy sauce, wasabi, oil and lime juice. Drizzle dressing over noodle mixture; toss gently to combine.

5 Divide noodles among serving plates; top with tuna and sprinkle with remaining onions.

NUTRITIONAL INFO PER SERVING 18g total fat (6g saturated fat); 70g carbohydrate; 64g protein; 4g fiber; 715 calories

shrimp, asparagus and sesame stir-fry

preparation time 30 minutes **cooking time** 15 minutes **serves** 4

2 pounds uncooked large shrimp

1 ½ tablespoons peanut oil

2-inch piece fresh ginger, grated

2 cloves garlic, crushed

1 medium onion, sliced thinly

10 ½ ounces asparagus, trimmed,
   chopped coarsely

1 jalapeño pepper, sliced thinly

3 tablespoons rice wine

¼ cup soy sauce

2 teaspoons sesame oil

2 teaspoons brown sugar

2 teaspoons toasted sesame seeds

1 Peel and devein shrimp, leaving tails intact.

2 Heat half of the peanut oil in wok or skillet; stir-fry ginger, garlic and onion until fragrant. Add asparagus; stir-fry until tender. Remove from pan.

3 Heat remaining peanut oil in same pan; cook shrimp, in batches, until cooked through. Return all shrimp to pan with asparagus mixture, jalapeño pepper and combined wine, soy sauce, sesame oil and sugar; stir-fry until mixture is heated through. Sprinkle with sesame seeds.

NUTRITIONAL INFO PER SERVING 9g total fat (1g saturated fat); 5g carbohydrate; 29g protein; 2g fiber; 217 calories

sweet and sour cod

preparation time 20 minutes **cooking time** 20 minutes **serves** 4

1 small pineapple (about 2 pounds),
   chopped coarsely

1 large red bell pepper, chopped coarsely

1 medium green bell pepper,
   chopped coarsely

1 medium red onion, sliced thinly

four 7-ounce cod fillets

3 tablespoons sugar

½ cup white vinegar

3 tablespoons soy sauce

1 serrano pepper, seeded, sliced thinly

1 ½-inch piece fresh ginger, grated

3 green onions, sliced thinly

1 Cook pineapple, bell peppers and red onion on heated lightly oiled grill pan or skillet until browned all over and tender.

2 In same pan, cook fish until cooked to desired degree of doneness.

3 Combine sugar, vinegar, soy sauce, serrano and ginger in large bowl. Place pineapple, bell peppers and red onion in bowl with dressing; toss gently to combine. Divide mixture among serving plates; top with fish and green onions.

NUTRITIONAL INFO PER SERVING 5g total fat (1g saturated fat); 26g carbohydrate; 45g protein; 5g fiber; 333 calories

pan-fried fish with roasted ratatouille

preparation time 20 minutes **cooking time** 35 minutes **serves** 4

Ratatouille is traditionally a stew of Mediterranean vegetables prepared on top of the stove. Here, we oven-roast them, and the effect is sensational.

3 large plum tomatoes, peeled,
   chopped coarsely
2 baby eggplants, sliced thickly
2 medium zucchini, sliced thickly
2 medium red bell peppers,
   chopped coarsely
1 medium red onion, cut into wedges
⅓ cup olive oil
2 cloves garlic, crushed
½ cup loosely packed torn fresh
   basil leaves
1 ½ tablespoons coarsely chopped
   fresh oregano
eight 4-ounce red snapper, tilapia or
   catfish fillets
2 cups baby spinach leaves

1 Preheat oven to 475°F.

2 Place tomatoes, eggplants, zucchini, bell peppers, onion and 1 ½ tablespoons of the oil in large baking dish; toss to coat vegetables. Roast, in single layer, uncovered, stirring occasionally, about 20 minutes or until vegetables are brown and tender. Stir in garlic and herbs.

3 Blend or process 2 cups of the vegetables with 1 ½ tablespoons of the remaining oil until smooth; cover to keep warm.

4 Heat remaining oil in large skillet; cook fish, in batches, about 2 minutes each side or until cooked to desired degree of doneness. Divide ratatouille puree among serving plates; top with vegetables, fish and spinach.

NUTRITIONAL INFO PER SERVING 21g total fat (4g saturated fat); 2g carbohydrate; 53g protein; 5g fiber; 475 calories

swordfish skewers with mashed potatoes and skordalia

preparation time 20 minutes (plus refrigeration time) **cooking time** 30 minutes **serves** 4

Skordalia is a Greek garlic sauce that is delicious on grilled fish and meats, used as a dip for vegetables, or stirred into soups.

1 ¾ pounds swordfish fillets,
   cut into ¾-inch pieces
¼ cup olive oil
3 tablespoons finely chopped fresh
   flat-leaf parsley
3 tablespoons finely chopped fresh thyme
1 pinch grated lemon peel
2 pounds baby potatoes, unpeeled
½ cup sour cream
3 tablespoons butter, softened

Skordalia
1 small potato
1 slice white bread
2 cloves garlic, crushed
1 ½ tablespoons apple cider vinegar
¼ cup water
3 tablespoons olive oil

1 Thread fish onto eight skewers; place in medium shallow dish. Brush with combined oil. herbs and lemon peel. Cover; refrigerate 20 minutes.

2 Make skordalia.

3 Boil, steam or microwave potatoes until tender; drain. Mash half the potatoes in medium bowl with sour cream and butter until smooth. Using fork, crush remaining potatoes until skins burst; fold into mash mixture. Cover to keep warm.

4 Cook skewers on heated oiled grill pan. Serve skewers with mashed potatoes and skordalia.

Skordalia Boil, steam or microwave potato until tender; drain. Mash potato in medium bowl until smooth. Discard crusts from bread. Soak bread in small bowl of cold water; drain. Squeeze out excess water. Blend or process bread with remaining ingredients until smooth. Stir bread mixture into potato.

Tip You'll need to soak eight bamboo skewers in cold water for at least an hour before use to prevent them from splintering and scorching.

NUTRITIONAL INFO PER SERVING 45g total fat (17g saturated fat); 40g carbohydrate; 43g protein; 5g fiber; 745 calories

tempura shrimp salad

preparation time 25 minutes **cooking time** 20 minutes **serves** 4

1-inch piece fresh ginger,
  chopped coarsely
¼ cup soy sauce
¼ cup mirin (rice wine)
2 tablespoons brown sugar
3 cucumbers
1 tablespoon drained sliced pickled ginger
1 small red onion, halved and sliced thinly
3 ounces baby arugula
1 egg, beaten lightly
½ cup cornstarch
½ cup all-purpose flour
¾ cup cold club soda
32 fresh medium shrimp (3 pounds),
  peeled and deveined with tails intact
vegetable oil, for deep-frying

1 Press fresh ginger through garlic press into screw-top jar, add soy sauce, mirin and sugar; shake dressing until sugar dissolves.

2 Using vegetable peeler, slice cucumbers lengthwise into thin strips. Cut pickled ginger slices into thin strips. Place cucumber and pickled ginger in large bowl with onion and arugula; toss gently to combine.

3 Combine egg, cornstarch, flour, and club soda in medium bowl, mixing lightly until just combined. Do not overmix (mixture should be lumpy). Let stand 5 minutes.

4 Heat oil in wok or large pot; dip prawns in batter, one at a time, draining away excess. Deep-fry shrimp, in batches, until lightly browned; drain on paper towels.

5 Pour half of the dressing over salad; toss gently to combine. Divide salad among serving plates, top with shrimp, and drizzle with remaining dressing.

NUTRITIONAL INFO PER SERVING 12g total fat (2g saturated fat); 40g carbohydrate; 44g protein; 2g fiber; 464 calories

salmon with spinach, fennel and apple salad

preparation time 20 minutes   **cooking time** 5 minutes   **serves** 4

3 tablespoons red wine vinegar

1 ½ tablespoons olive oil

2 teaspoons sugar

2 teaspoons Dijon mustard

four 7-ounce salmon steaks

1 ½ tablespoons finely chopped
   fresh chives

1 ½ tablespoons finely chopped fresh dill

7 cups baby spinach leaves

2 medium apples, sliced thinly

2 baby fennel bulbs, trimmed, sliced thinly

1 small cucumber, seeded, sliced thinly

½ cup coarsely chopped fresh chives

¼ cup coarsely chopped fresh dill

1 Whisk together vinegar, oil, sugar and mustard.

2 Combine 1½ tablespoons of the dressing with fish, chives and dill in medium bowl; toss fish to coat in mixture. Cook fish in large, heated, lightly oiled skillet until cooked to desired degree of doneness.

3 Place remaining ingredients in large bowl with remaining dressing; toss gently to combine. Serve fish with salad.

NUTRITIONAL INFO PER SERVING 19g total fat (4g saturated fat); 11g carbohydrate; 41g protein; 4g fiber; 379 calories

Moroccan spiced fish with couscous

preparation time 20 minutes **cooking time** 15 minutes **serves** 4

1 clove garlic, crushed

½-inch piece fresh ginger, grated finely

1 teaspoon ground cumin

½ teaspoon ground turmeric

½ teaspoon hot paprika

½ teaspoon ground coriander

four ½-pound halibut or other firm
   white fish fillets

1 tablespoon olive oil

Couscous

2 cups couscous

2 cups boiling water

¼ cup butter

1 large pear, chopped finely

½ cup finely chopped dried apricots

½ cup coarsely chopped dried figs

½ cup coarsely chopped fresh
   flat-leaf parsley

¼ cup toasted pine nuts

1 Combine garlic, ginger, and spices in large bowl. Add fish, tossing to coat.

2 Heat oil in large skillet; cook fish, in batches, until browned on both sides and cooked to desired degree of doneness.

3 Make couscous.

4 Divide couscous among serving plates; top with fish. Serve with a bowl of yogurt and mixed with chopped fresh cilantro, if desired.

Couscous Combine couscous, 2 cups boiling water, and butter in large heatproof bowl; cover, and let stand about 5 minutes or until water is absorbed. Fluff with fork. Stir in remaining ingredients.

NUTRITIONAL INFO PER SERVING 27g total fat (9g saturated fat); 11g carbohydrate; 57g protein; 9g fiber; 927 calories

salmon phyllo triangles

preparation time 15 minutes **cooking time** 15 minutes **serves** 4

1 ½ tablespoons butter

3 green onions, sliced thinly

1 small red bell pepper, chopped finely

3 tablespoons all-purpose flour

¼ cup milk

½ cup heavy cream

1 ½ tablespoons fresh lemon juice

1 ½ tablespoons drained baby capers,
  rinsed

1 cup baby spinach

14-ounce can red salmon, drained, flaked

4 sheets phyllo pastry, thawed

4 tablespoons butter, melted

5 cups mixed salad greens

7 ounces cherry tomatoes, halved

1 Melt butter in medium skillet; cook onions and bell pepper, stirring, until onion softens. Add flour; cook, stirring, until mixture bubbles. Gradually add combined milk and cream; stir until mixture boils and thickens. Remove from heat; stir in lemon juice, capers, spinach and salmon.

2 Preheat oven to 400°F.

3 Brush one sheet of the phyllo with a little of the melted butter; fold in half lengthwise. Place a quarter of the salmon mixture at bottom of one narrow edge of phyllo, leaving a ½-inch border. Fold opposite corner of phyllo diagonally across filling to form a triangle; continue folding to end of phyllo piece, retaining triangle shape. Place triangle on lightly greased baking sheet, seam-side down; repeat with remaining phyllo and salmon mixture.

4 Brush triangles with remaining melted butter; bake, uncovered, about 10 minutes or until browned lightly and heated through.

5 Serve with a salad of mixed greens and tomatoes.

NUTRITIONAL INFO PER SERVING 39g total fat (22g saturated fat); 19g carbohydrate; 23g protein; 3g fiber; 522 calories

halibut with tomato, caper and walnut dressing

preparation time 15 minutes **cooking time** 20 minutes **serves** 4

four 6 ½-ounce halibut fillets

Tomato, caper and walnut dressing
8 ounces cherry tomatoes
5 tablespoons butter
1 ½ tablespoons finely grated lemon peel
2 teaspoons fresh lemon juice
1 teaspoon drained capers, rinsed,
    chopped finely
¼ cup finely chopped walnuts
½ cup coarsely chopped fresh
    flat-leaf parsley

1 Make tomato, caper and walnut dressing.
2 Cook fish on heated oiled grill pan or grill until cooked to desired degree of doneness. Serve fish topped with dressing.

Tomato, caper and walnut dressing Cook tomatoes on heated oiled grill pan until tender. Melt butter in small pot; add tomatoes and remaining ingredients, stirring until hot.

NUTRITIONAL INFO PER SERVING 20g total fat (9g saturated fat); 2g carbohydrate; 40g protein; 2g fiber; 352 calories

salmon with garlic ginger butter

preparation time 10 minutes **cooking time** 10 minutes **serves** 6

6 salmon fillets (3 pounds)

1 stick plus 2 tablespoons butter, chopped

3 tablespoons soy sauce

2 cloves garlic, crushed

2-inch piece fresh ginger, grated

1 ½ tablespoons brown sugar

1 teaspoon finely grated lemon peel

3 tablespoons fresh lemon juice

1 Cook salmon on heated oiled grill pan or skillet until cooked to desired degree of doneness.

2 Stir remaining ingredients in small pot over low heat until butter melts.

3 Spoon butter mixture over salmon and serve with steamed rice and baby bok choy.

NUTRITIONAL INFO PER SERVING 36g total fat (17g saturated fat); 3g carbohydrate; 44g protein; 1g fiber; 509 calories

Beef & Veal

Enjoying a juicy, grilled steak is one of life's simple pleasures. Beef makes dinner a special occasion, whether it's a cozy weeknight supper or a festive dinner party.

steaks with blue cheese butter and pear salad

preparation time 15 minutes   **cooking time** 10 minutes   **serves** 4

4 porterhouse or t-bone steaks
   (3 ½ pounds)
3 tablespoons olive oil
2 ounces blue cheese, at room temperature
4 tablespoons butter, softened
2 green onions, chopped finely
1 ½ tablespoons whole-grain mustard
1 teaspoon honey
¼ cup olive oil
1 ½ tablespoons red wine vinegar
3 ½ ounces mixed salad greens
1 ripe pear, sliced thinly
½ cup roasted pecans

1 Brush steaks with oil; season both sides with salt and pepper. Cook on heated oiled grill pan or skillet until browned on both sides and cooked to desired degree of doneness.

2 Combine cheese, butter and onions in small bowl.

3 Whisk together mustard, honey, ¼ cup oil and vinegar.

4 Place salad greens, pear and nuts in medium bowl with honey mustard dressing; toss gently to combine.

5 Spread blue-cheese butter on hot beef; serve with salad.

NUTRITIONAL INFO PER SERVING 66g total fat (20g saturated fat); 9g carbohydrate; 59g protein; 3g fiber; 853 calories

beef tenderloin with horseradish herb crust and arugula salad

preparation time 20 minutes (plus refrigeration time) **cooking time** 50 minutes (plus standing time) **serves** 6

¼ cup prepared horseradish

1 ½ tablespoons olive oil

2-pound piece beef tenderloin

3 tablespoons whole-grain mustard

1 ½ tablespoons coarsely chopped
   fresh flat-leaf parsley

½ cup fresh breadcrumbs

1 ½ tablespoons butter, melted

Arugula salad

3 ½ cups baby arugula

1 medium red onion, sliced thinly

8 green onions, sliced thinly

¼ cup roasted pine nuts

⅓ cup balsamic vinegar

⅓ cup olive oil

1 Combine horseradish and oil in large bowl; add beef, turn to coat in mixture. Cover; refrigerate 3 hours or overnight.

2 Sear beef in heated oiled skillet or grill pan, turning, until browned all over. Reduce heat; cook beef, turning occasionally, about 30 minutes or until cooked. Cover, let stand 10 minutes.

3 Make arugula salad.

4 Preheat broiler.

5 Combine mustard, parsley and breadcrumbs in small bowl with half the butter. Brush beef with remaining butter; press breadcrumb mixture onto beef. Broil beef until crust is browned. Let stand 10 minutes; slice thickly.

6 Serve beef with arugula salad.

Arugula salad Place ingredients in large bowl; toss gently to combine.

Tip Be sure to use prepared white horseradish, not cream-style horseradish for this recipe.

NUTRITIONAL INFO PER SERVING 34g total fat (9g saturated fat); 9g carbohydrate; 38g protein; 2g fiber; 498 calories

hamburger with a twist

preparation time 15 minutes **cooking time** 10 minutes **serves** 4

3 ounces gorgonzola or other blue cheese, crumbled

¼ cup sour cream

14 ounces ground beef

4 ounces ground sausage

1 small onion, chopped finely

1 ½ tablespoons barbecue sauce

2 teaspoons Worcestershire sauce

½ cup drained sun-dried tomatoes in oil, chopped finely

4 hamburger buns

2 cups baby arugula

6 ounces marinated artichoke hearts, drained, quartered

1 Blend or process half of the cheese with the cream until smooth. Stir in remaining cheese.

2 Using hands, combine meats, onion, sauces and tomatoes in medium bowl; shape mixture into four hamburger patties.

3 Cook patties in large, heated, lightly oiled skillet until browned on both sides and cooked through.

4 Toast buns, layer arugula, burgers, gorgonzola cream and artichokes.

NUTRITIONAL INFO PER SERVING 30g total fat (15g saturated fat); 39g carbohydrate; 36g protein; 6g fiber; 584 calories

honey barbecued steak

preparation time 15 minutes **cooking time** 10 minutes **serves** 4

2 tablespoons barbecue sauce

1 tablespoon Worcestershire sauce

1 tablespoon honey

1 fresh serrano pepper, chopped finely
  (optional)

1 clove garlic, crushed

four 6-ounce strip steaks

1 Combine barbecue sauce, Worcestershire sauce, honey, serrano, and garlic in large bowl; add steaks, turning to coat.

2 Cook steaks on grill pan (or grill) until browned on both sides and cooked to desired degree of doneness.

3 Serve steaks with coleslaw.

NUTRITIONAL INFO PER SERVING 12g total fat (5g saturated fat); 12g carbohydrate; 42g protein; 1g fiber; 324 calories

New York strip steaks with lemon thyme butter

preparation time 15 minutes (plus refrigeration time) **cooking time** 45 minutes **serves** 4

4 large potatoes (about 2½ pounds),
 cut into wedges
2 medium red onions, cut into wedges
1 medium lemon, cut into wedges
2 teaspoons fresh thyme
¼ cup olive oil
4 New York strip steaks (2 pounds)

Lemon thyme butter
5 tablespoons butter, softened
2 teaspoons finely grated lemon peel
1 teaspoon finely chopped fresh thyme
1 clove garlic, crushed

1 Preheat oven to 425°F.

2 Make lemon thyme butter.

3 Combine potatoes, onions, lemon, thyme and oil in large deep baking dish. Roast, uncovered, stirring occasionally, about 45 minutes or until potatoes are browned and crisp.

4 Cook steaks, in batches, on heated oiled grill or skillet until browned on both sides and cooked to desired degree of doneness.

5 Serve steaks with potatoes topped with lemon thyme butter.

Lemon thyme butter Combine ingredients in small bowl. Cover; refrigerate until firm.

Tip For an elegant presentation, place lemon thyme butter on a large sheet of plastic wrap. Form into a fat cylinder and roll up in the plastic wrap, pushing and tucking in as you go to form a tight log. Refrigerate until needed, unwrap and slice into disks.

NUTRITIONAL INFO PER SERVING 46g total fat (19g saturated fat); 39g carbohydrate; 54g protein; 6g fiber; 796 calories

steak sandwich with tarragon and tomato salsa

preparation time 15 minutes **cooking time** 15 minutes **serves** 4

Use ciabatta, focaccia or country bread for this recipe.

four ¼-pound rib eye steaks
2 cloves garlic, crushed
1 tablespoon Dijon mustard
1 tablespoon olive oil
8 thick slices bread
⅓ cup mayonnaise
1 ounce trimmed watercress

Tarragon and tomato salsa
2 cloves garlic, crushed
3 large Roma tomatoes, quartered and thinly sliced
½ small red onion, sliced thinly
1 tablespoon finely chopped fresh tarragon

1 Combine steaks, garlic, mustard and 1 ½ teaspoons of the oil in medium bowl.

2 Make tarragon and tomato salsa.

3 Grill steaks on grill pan or skillet until desired degree of doneness. Remove from heat, cover; let stand 5 minutes.

4 Brush both sides of bread with remaining oil; toast on grill pan or skillet. Spread one side of each slice with mayonnaise, and top with watercress, steak and salsa; top with remaining bread slices.

Tarragon and tomato salsa Combine ingredients in medium bowl.

NUTRITIONAL INFO PER SERVING 22g total fat (5g saturated fat); 43g carbohydrate; 35g protein; 4g fiber; 517 calories

steak diane

preparation time 10 minutes **cooking time** 15 minutes **serves** 4

1 ½ tablespoons olive oil

8 thin slices beef tenderloin (1 ¾ pounds)

1 ½ tablespoons butter

3 cloves garlic, crushed

3 green onions, sliced thinly

1 ½ tablespoons brandy

3 tablespoons Worcestershire sauce

1 ½ cups heavy cream

1 Heat oil in large skillet; cook beef, in batches, until browned on both sides and cooked as desired. Cover to keep warm.

2 Melt butter in same skillet; cook garlic and onions, stirring, until onions soften. Add brandy and sauce; bring to a boil. Stir in cream, reduce heat; simmer, uncovered, about 3 minutes or until sauces thickens slightly.

3 Divide beef among serving plates; top with sauce.

NUTRITIONAL INFO PER SERVING 53g total fat (30g saturated fat); 5g carbohydrate; 44g protein; 1g fiber; 680 calories

chili t-bones with hash browns

preparation time 15 minutes (plus refrigeration time) **cooking time** 20 minutes **serves** 4

4 t-bone steaks (2 ½ pounds)

⅓ cup Worcestershire sauce

⅓ cup hot chili sauce

3 medium potatoes (about 1 ¼ pounds)

3 tablespoons butter

1 small onion, chopped finely

2 slices bacon (3 ounces), chopped finely

1 Combine steaks and sauces in large bowl; toss to coat steaks in marinade. Cover; refrigerate 20 minutes.

2 Grate potatoes coarsely. Squeeze excess liquid from potatoes by hand; spread onto sheets of paper towels, squeeze again to remove as much liquid as possible from potatoes.

3 Heat half of the butter in large non-stick skillet; cook onion and bacon, stirring, until onion softens. Add potatoes; stir over medium heat constantly until potatoes begin to stick to skillet. Remove from heat; cool 5 minutes. Transfer potato mixture to large bowl.

4 Using wet hands, shape potato mixture into eight patties. Heat remaining butter in same skillet; cook hash browns again, in batches, until browned and crisp on both sides. Drain on paper towels.

5 Drain steaks; discard marinade. Cook steaks, in batches, on heated oiled grill pan or skillet until browned on both sides and cooked to desired degree of doneness.

NUTRITIONAL INFO PER SERVING 23g total fat (11g saturated fat); 29g carbohydrate; 48g protein; 4g fiber; 521 calories

filet mignon with caramelized shallots and mashed potatoes

preparation time 20 minutes **cooking time** 40 minutes **serves** 4

2 pounds potatoes, chopped coarsely
4 tablespoons butter, chopped
½ cup heavy cream
16 shallots
3 green onions
2 teaspoons olive oil
1 ½ tablespoons butter
1 teaspoon brown sugar
⅓ cup dry red wine
2 cups beef stock
four 5-ounce filet mignon steaks

1 Boil, steam or microwave potatoes until tender; drain. Push potatoes through sieve into large bowl, add butter and cream; mash. Cover to keep warm.

2 Peel shallots leaving roots intact; cut green onions into 3-inch lengths. Heat oil and 1 ½ tablespoons of butter in medium skillet; cook shallots and green onions, stirring, until shallots are browned lightly and softened.

3 Remove green onions from skillet; reserve. Add sugar to skillet; cook over low heat, stirring, about 10 minutes or until shallots are caramelized.

4 Add wine and stock to skillet; bring to a boil. Reduce heat; simmer, uncovered, about 10 minutes or until mixture thickens slightly. Return green onions to skillet; simmer, uncovered, 2 minutes.

5 Cook beef on heated oiled grill pan or skillet until browned on both sides and cooked to desired degree of doneness.

6 Divide beef, mashed potatoes and shallot mixture among serving plates; drizzle with remaining shallot sauce.

NUTRITIONAL INFO PER SERVING 40 total fat (23g saturated fat); 34g carbohydrate; 41g protein; 4g fiber; 676 calories

steaks with mashed parsnips and potatoes

preparation time 10 minutes (plus marinating time) **cooking time** 20 minutes **serves** 4

4 New York strip or sirloin steaks
  (2 pounds)
½ cup plum sauce
⅓ cup tomato sauce
⅓ cup Worcestershire sauce
2 cloves garlic, crushed
2 green onions, chopped finely
2 pounds potatoes, chopped coarsely
2 medium parsnips, chopped coarsely
3 tablespoons butter, chopped
⅓ cup heavy cream
8 cups baby spinach

1 Combine steaks in large bowl with sauces, garlic and onions; toss to coat steaks in marinade. Cover; refrigerate 30 minutes.

2 Boil, steam or microwave potatoes and parsnips together until just tender; drain. Mash with butter and cream in large bowl until smooth. Cover to keep warm.

3 Drain steaks; discard marinade. Cook steaks on heated oiled grill pan or skillet until browned on both sides and cooked to desired degree of doneness.

4 Boil, steam or microwave spinach until just wilted; drain.

5 Serve steaks with spinach, and mashed parsnips and potatoes.

NUTRITIONAL INFO PER SERVING 31g total fat (17g saturated fat); 67g carbohydrate; 55g protein; 8g fiber; 784 calories

Moroccan beef with citrus couscous

preparation time 15 minutes (plus standing time) **cooking time** 20 minutes **serves** 4

2 cloves garlic, crushed

1 teaspoon ground ginger

1 ½ tablespoons ground cumin

2 teaspoons ground coriander

1-pound piece rump roast

1 ½ tablespoons harissa

1 cup beef stock

7 ounces pitted green olives,
  crushed slightly

½ cup coarsely chopped fresh cilantro

Citrus couscous

2 medium oranges (about 1 pound)

1 cup water

1 cup fresh orange juice

2 cups couscous

¼ cup roasted slivered almonds

1 ½ tablespoons thinly sliced
  preserved lemon

1 small red onion, sliced thinly

1 pound red radishes, trimmed,
  sliced thinly

1 Combine garlic and spices in medium bowl; reserve about a third of the spice mixture. Add beef to bowl with remaining two-thirds of the spice mixture; toss to coat beef all over. Cook beef on heated oiled grill pan or skillet until browned on all sides and cooked to degree of desired doneness. Cover; let stand 10 minutes.

2 Make citrus couscous.

3 Cook harissa and remaining spice mixture in dry, small, heated non-stick skillet until fragrant. Add stock; bring to a boil. Reduce heat; simmer, uncovered, about 3 minutes or until harissa sauce reduces by half. Remove from heat; stir in olives and cilantro. Serve sliced beef on couscous, drizzle with warm dressing.

Citrus couscous Remove skin and white pith from oranges; cut in half, slice thinly. Place the water and orange juice in medium pot; bring to a boil. Remove from heat; stir in couscous. Cover; let stand about 5 minutes or until liquid is absorbed. Fluff with fork. Add orange and remaining ingredients; toss gently to combine.

Tips Preserved lemons, a prominent ingredient in North African cooking, are lemons which have been bottled in salt and oil for several months; their flavor is subtle and perfumed. Rinse the lemons well then remove and discard flesh, using the peel only. While available in some Middle Eastern markets, they can be difficult to find in the United States. Make your own by cutting several slits in a lemon and packing them with salt; wrap the lemon in plastic wrap and refrigerate for 24 hours. Harissa is a Moroccan chili paste available in Asian or Middle Eastern markets.

NUTRITIONAL INFO PER SERVING 15g total fat (4g saturated fat); 105g carbohydrate; 47g protein; 6g fiber; 758 calories

filet mignon stuffed with spinach, cheese and pepper with parmesan mashed potatoes

preparation time 20 minutes **cooking time** 15 minutes **serves** 4

1 medium red bell pepper
2 pounds potatoes, chopped coarsely
4 filet mignon steaks (1 pound)
4 thick slices gouda cheese (4 ounces)
1 cup baby spinach
¼ cup heavy cream
1 ½ tablespoons butter
½ cup finely grated parmesan cheese
14 ounces sugar snap peas

1 Quarter bell pepper; remove seeds and membranes. Roast bell pepper under broiler or in 475°F oven, skin-side up, until skin blisters and blackens. Cover with plastic or foil for 5 minutes. Peel away skin.

2 Boil, steam or microwave potatoes until tender; drain. Cover to keep warm.

3 Preheat oven to 425°F.

4 Cut steaks in half horizontally; divide gouda cheese, spinach and bell pepper among four steak halves, cover with remaining steak halves. Tie stacks with kitchen string; cook, uncovered, in large, oiled non-stick skillet until browned on both sides. Transfer to baking sheet; cook, uncovered, in oven about 10 minutes or until cooked to desired degree of doneness.

5 Mash potatoes with cream, butter and parmesan cheese until smooth. Boil, steam or microwave peas until just tender; drain.

6 Serve stacks with parmesan potatoes and peas.

NUTRITIONAL INFO PER SERVING 32g total fat (18g saturated fat); 4g carbohydrate; 48g protein; 6g fiber; 624 calories

potato wedges with sloppy joe topping

preparation time 10 minutes **cooking time** 30 minutes **serves** 4

4 medium russet or Idaho potatoes
   (about 1 ¾ pounds)
3 tablespoons olive oil
1 clove garlic, crushed
1 large onion, chopped finely
1 small green bell pepper, chopped finely
1 celery stalk, chopped finely
1 ¾ pounds ground beef
3 tablespoons yellow mustard
3 tablespoons cider vinegar
1 cup tomato sauce
½ cup coarsely grated cheddar cheese
2 green onions, sliced thinly

1 Preheat oven to 425°F.
2 Cut each potato into eight wedges; place in large shallow baking dish, drizzle with half of the oil. Roast, uncovered, about 30 minutes or until wedges are tender.
3 Heat remaining oil in large skillet; cook garlic, onion, bell pepper and celery, stirring, until vegetables soften. Add beef; cook, stirring, until changed in color. Stir in mustard, vinegar and sauce; bring to a boil. Reduce heat; cook, stirring, until meat is cooked through and sauce is slightly thickened.
4 Serve wedges topped with sloppy joe mixture; sprinkle with cheese and onions.

NUTRITIONAL INFO PER SERVING 27g total fat (9g saturated fat); 42g carbohydrate; 49g protein; 6g fiber; 613 calories

Sicilian stuffed pizza

preparation time 20 minutes **cooking time** 35 minutes (plus standing time) **serves** 4

Called sfinciuni or sfincione in Sicily, we call it delicious — a double-decker pizza with its aromatic filling hidden between the layers.

¾ cup warm water

1 ½ teaspoons dried yeast

½ teaspoon sugar

2 cups all-purpose flour

1 teaspoon salt

⅓ cup olive oil

1 cup breadcrumbs

2 cloves garlic, crushed

1 teaspoon ground fennel seeds

1 small red onion, chopped finely

8 ounces ground beef

3 ½ ounces Italian salami, chopped finely

14 ½-ounce can crushed tomatoes,
   undrained

¼ cup pine nuts, toasted

¼ cup coarsely chopped fresh
   flat-leaf parsley

½ cup finely grated fontina cheese

1 Combine the water, yeast and sugar in small bowl, cover; let stand in warm place about 15 minutes or until frothy. Combine flour and salt in large bowl, stir in yeast mixture and half of the oil; mix to a soft dough. Turn dough onto lightly floured surface, knead about 5 minutes or until smooth and elastic. Place dough in large lightly oiled bowl, cover; let stand in warm place about 1 hour or until dough doubles in size.

2 Meanwhile, heat remaining oil in large skillet; cook breadcrumbs and half of the garlic, stirring, until crumbs are browned lightly. Remove from skillet.

3 Reheat same skillet; cook fennel, onion and remaining garlic, stirring, until onion just softens. Add beef; cook, stirring, until beef changes color. Stir in salami and undrained tomatoes; bring to a boil. Reduce heat; simmer, uncovered, stirring occasionally, about 15 minutes or until liquid reduces by half. Remove from heat; stir in nuts and parsley. Cool.

4 Preheat oven to 425°F.

5 Knead dough on lightly floured surface until smooth; divide in half. Roll each half into 12-inch round. Place one round on lightly greased pizza or baking sheet, top with breadcrumb mixture, beef mixture, cheese and remaining round. Pinch edges together; bake, uncovered, about 15 minutes or until browned lightly.

6 Let pizza stand 10 minutes before cutting into wedges and serving with an arugula and parmesan salad, if desired.

Tip You can use your favorite pre-made pizza dough if desired.

NUTRITIONAL INFO PER SERVING 46.8g total fat (11.4g saturated fat); 72.4g carbohydrate; 35.3g protein; 6.5g fiber; 864 calories

kofta with fresh green onion couscous

preparation time 20 minutes (plus refrigeration time) **cooking time** 15 minutes **serves** 4

Kofta is a delicious Middle Eastern dish of spiced meatballs cooked on skewers. Soak 12 bamboo skewers in cold water for at least an hour before use to prevent splintering and scorching.

2 pounds ground beef

1 medium onion, chopped finely

2 cloves garlic, crushed

3 tablespoons fresh lemon juice

1 ½ teaspoons ground cumin

1 ½ teaspoons ground coriander

¼ cup toasted pine nuts

3 tablespoons finely chopped fresh mint

1 ½ tablespoons finely chopped
   fresh cilantro

1 egg

2 cups beef stock

2 cups couscous

2 tablespoons butter, chopped

2 green onions, sliced thinly

1 Combine beef, onion, garlic, lemon juice, spices, nuts, herbs and egg by hand in large bowl; roll heaping tablespoons of mixture into balls, thread three balls on each skewer. Place kofta skewers on tray, cover; refrigerate 30 minutes.

2 Place stock in medium pot; bring to a boil. Remove from heat, add couscous and butter, cover; let stand about 5 minutes or until stock is absorbed. Fluff with a fork.

3 Cook kofta on heated oiled grill pan or skillet until browned all over and cooked through.

4 Toss green onions with couscous; serve with kofta, accompanied by a bowl of yogurt mixed with chopped cucumber, if desired.

NUTRITIONAL INFO PER SERVING 33g total fat (12g saturated fat); 81g carbohydrate; 69g protein; 2g fiber; 901 calories

souvlaki with Greek salad

preparation time 30 minutes (plus marinating time) **cooking time** 15 minutes **serves** 4

Souvlaki is a Greek specialty: delectably tender meat skewers which have been marinated in an herb, lemon and olive oil mixture. Soak 8 bamboo skewers in cold water for at least an hour before use to prevent splintering and scorching.

1 ¾ pounds boneless sirloin or
    filet mignon steak, cut into ¾-inch cubes
1 large onion, cut into wedges
¼ cup olive oil
¼ cup fresh lemon juice
1 ½ tablespoons dried oregano

Greek salad

4 medium plum tomatoes,
    chopped coarsely
2 small cucumbers, chopped coarsely
1 small red onion, sliced thinly
1 large green bell pepper,
    chopped coarsely
½ cup pitted kalamata olives
5 ounces feta cheese, chopped coarsely
1 ½ tablespoons olive oil
1 ½ tablespoons fresh lemon juice
2 teaspoons fresh oregano

1 Thread steak and onion alternately on skewers; place souvlaki, in single layer, in large shallow dish. Combine oil, lemon juice and oregano in measuring cup; pour over souvlaki. Cover; refrigerate 3 hours or overnight.

2 Make Greek salad.

3 Cook souvlaki, in batches, on heated oiled grill or grill pan until browned all over and cooked as desired. Serve souvlaki and Greek salad with yogurt mixed with chopped cucumber, if desired.

Greek salad Combine tomatoes, cucumbers, onion, bell pepper, olives and cheese in large bowl. Whisk together remaining ingredients. Pour dressing over salad in bowl; toss gently to combine.

NUTRITIONAL INFO PER SERVING 40g total fat (14g saturated fat); 14g carbohydrate; 52g protein; 4g fiber; 629 calories

basil and oregano steak with grilled vegetables

preparation time 20 minutes **cooking time** 30 minutes **serves** 4

2 teaspoons finely chopped fresh oregano

¼ cup finely chopped fresh basil

1 ½ tablespoons finely grated lemon peel

3 tablespoons fresh lemon juice

4 drained anchovy fillets, chopped finely

four 7-ounce beef sirloin steaks

2 baby fennel bulbs, quartered

3 small zucchini, chopped coarsely

1 large red bell pepper, sliced thickly

7 ounces portobello mushrooms, sliced thickly

4 baby eggplants, chopped coarsely

2 small red onions, sliced thickly

2 teaspoons olive oil

¼ cup fresh lemon juice

3 tablespoons fresh oregano

1 Combine chopped oregano, basil, lemon peel, lemon juice and anchovies in large bowl, add beef; toss beef to coat in marinade. Cover; refrigerate until needed.
2 Combine fennel, zucchini, bell pepper, mushrooms, eggplants, onions and oil in large bowl; cook vegetables, in batches, on heated lightly oiled grill or grill pan until just tender. Add lemon juice and oregano leaves to bowl with vegetables; toss gently to combine. Cover to keep warm.
3 Cook beef mixture on same grill or pan until cooked to degree of desired doneness; serve with vegetables.

Tip Baby eggplants and fennel, like most other baby vegetables, are sweeter and more tender than their adult counterparts, making them most desireable for simple and delicious results.

NUTRITIONAL INFO PER SERVING 26g total fat (11g saturated fat); 71g carbohydrate; 58g protein; 6g fiber; 522 calories

fajitas and guacamole

preparation time 15 minutes (plus marinating time) **cooking time** 20 minutes **serves** 4

1 ¼ pounds rump roast or skirt steak

2 cloves garlic, crushed

¼ cup fresh lemon juice

1 ½ teaspoons ground cumin

½ teaspoon cayenne pepper

3 tablespoons olive oil

1 medium yellow bell pepper

1 medium red bell pepper

12 small flour tortillas

13-ounce jar chunky salsa

Guacamole

2 medium avocados (about 1 pound)

2 medium tomatoes, seeded, chopped finely

1 small red onion, chopped finely

3 tablespoons fresh lime juice

3 tablespoons coarsely chopped fresh cilantro

1 Cut beef into thin ¾-inch-wide slices; place in medium bowl with garlic, lemon juice, spices and oil, toss to coat beef in marinade. Cover; refrigerate.

2 Quarter bell peppers; remove seeds and membranes. Roast bell pepper under broiler or in 475°F oven, skin-side up, until skin blisters and blackens. Cover with plastic wrap or foil for 5 minutes. Peel away skin; cut bell peppers into thin strips.

3 Cook beef, in batches, on heated oiled grill pan or skillet until browned all over and cooked as desired; cover to keep warm. Reheat bell pepper strips on same heated pan.

4 Make guacamole.

5 Serve beef and bell pepper, with warmed tortillas, guacamole and salsa.

Guacamole Mash avocados roughly in medium bowl; add remaining ingredients, mix to combine.

Tip If possible, marinate steak the night before serving so the flavors can penetrate the meat.

NUTRITIONAL INFO PER SERVING 42g total fat (10g saturated fat); 42g carbohydrate; 42g protein; 7g fiber; 726 calories

Mexican spiced steak and chili beans

preparation time 25 minutes (plus standing time) **cooking time** 1 hour 20 minutes **serves** 4

2 pasilla chilies

¼ cup boiling water

3 tablespoons olive oil

1 medium onion, chopped finely

3 cloves garlic, crushed

¼ cup tomato paste

4 medium tomatoes (1 ¼ pounds), chopped coarsely

½ cup water

3 tablespoons fresh lime juice

3 tablespoons brown sugar

2 cans black beans

1 ½ tablespoons dried marjoram

2 teaspoons smoked paprika

2 pounds beef round steak

8 large flour tortillas

1 small head iceberg lettuce, trimmed, shredded

⅔ cup sour cream

1 small red onion, sliced thinly

⅓ cup firmly packed fresh cilantro

1 Soak chilies in ¼ cup of boiling water in small bowl 20 minutes; blend or process mixture until smooth.

2 Heat half the oil in large pot; cook onion and garlic, stirring, until onion softens. Add chili mixture, tomato paste, tomatoes, ½ cup of water, lime juice and sugar; bring to a boil. Remove from heat; blend or process until smooth.

3 Return chili mixture to pot; add beans, simmer, covered, 20 minutes. Uncover; simmer about 10 minutes or until sauce thickens.

4 Combine marjoram, paprika and remaining oil in large bowl; add beef, turn to coat in mixture. Cook beef, on both sides, on heated oiled grill pan until cooked to desired degree of doneness. Cover; let stand 10 minutes, slice thinly.

5 Divide tortillas into two batches; wrap each batch in a double thickness of foil. Heat tortillas, turning occasionally, on grill pan or skillet about 5 minutes or until warm. Serve tortillas with chili beans, beef, lettuce, sour cream, red onion and cilantro.

Tip Pasilla chilies, also called "chile negro" because of their dark brown color, are the wrinkled, dried version of fresh chilaca chilies. About 8-inch in length, a pasilla is only mildly hot, but possesses a rich flavor that adds smoky depth to the overall recipe.

NUTRITIONAL INFO PER SERVING 50g total fat (20g saturated fat); 96g carbohydrate; 92g protein; 21g fiber; 1234 calories

Thai beef patties with noodle salad

preparation time 20 minutes **cooking time** 10 minutes **serves** 4

8 ounces dried rice stick noodles

1 ¾ pounds ground beef

¼ cup red curry paste

3 tablespoons vegetable oil

8 ounces cherry tomatoes, halved

1 cucumber, halved, seeded, sliced thinly

4 green onions, chopped finely

1 medium red bell pepper, sliced thinly

1 cup bean sprouts

½ cup firmly packed fresh cilantro

½ cup sweet Thai chili sauce

¼ cup rice vinegar

1 Place noodles in large heatproof bowl, cover with boiling water, let stand until noodles just soften; drain.

2 Combine beef and curry paste by hand in medium bowl; shape mixture into 12 patties.

3 Heat oil in large skillet; cook patties, in batches, until browned on both sides and cooked through.

4 Combine tomatoes, cucumber, onions, bell pepper, sprouts and cilantro in large bowl. Add noodles and half of the combined chili sauce and vinegar; toss gently to combine.

5 Serve patties with noodle salad, drizzled with remaining dressing.

Tip Patties can be shaped several hours ahead and refrigerated, covered, until ready to cook.

NUTRITIONAL INFO PER SERVING 28g total fat (7g saturated fat); 25g carbohydrate; 47g protein; 6g fiber; 555 calories

beef coconut curry

preparation time 15 minutes **cooking time** 20 minutes **serves** 4

3 tablespoons peanut oil

1 pound rump roast, sliced thinly

1 medium onion, sliced thinly

2 teaspoons grated fresh ginger

1 clove garlic, crushed

⅓ cup mild curry paste

1 ⅔ cups coconut milk

1 medium yellow bell pepper, sliced thinly

5 ounces green beans, halved

1 Heat half of the oil in wok or large skillet; stir-fry beef, in batches, until browned all over.

2 Heat remaining oil in same wok; stir-fry onion until soft. Add ginger, garlic and curry paste; stir-fry until fragrant.

3 Stir in coconut milk; bring to a boil. Return beef to wok with bell pepper and beans; stir-fry until vegetables are just tender.

NUTRITIONAL INFO PER SERVING 46g total fat (24g saturated fat); 10g carbohydrate; 33g protein; 6g fiber; 596 calories

steak teriyaki

preparation time 10 minutes (plus marinating time) **cooking time** 10 minutes **serves** 4

1 ¾ pounds piece boneless sirloin or
   filet mignon steak, sliced thinly
¼ cup rice vinegar
¼ cup kecap manis
1 ½ tablespoons brown sugar
¼ cup fresh lime juice
1 clove garlic, crushed
2 small fresh red chilies, seeded,
   chopped finely (optional)
1 teaspoon sesame oil
1 ½ tablespoons peanut oil
2 large carrots, cut into matchsticks
7 ounces cabbage, shredded finely

1 Combine steak, vinegar, kecap manis, sugar, lime juice, garlic, chilies and sesame oil in large bowl, cover; refrigerate 3 hours or overnight. Drain steak; reserve marinade.

2 Heat peanut oil in wok or large skillet; stir-fry steak, in batches, until browned all over. Cover steak to keep warm.

3 Pour reserved marinade into wok; bring to a boil. Boil, uncovered, until sauce reduces by a third. Divide combined carrots and cabbage among serving plates; top with steak, drizzle with sauce. Serve with steamed rice.

Tip You can find kecap manis at Asian markets, or you can make your own by heating equal parts soy sauce and molasses or brown sugar, stirring until molasses or sugar dissolves.

NUTRITIONAL INFO PER SERVING 18g total fat (7g saturated fat); 11g carbohydrate; 44g protein; 4g fiber; 392 calories

five-spice ginger beef

preparation time 20 minutes **cooking time** 15 minutes **serves** 4

¼ cup peanut oil

4 cups coarsely shredded Chinese
  cabbage

½ cup coarsely chopped fresh chives

1 ¾ pounds sirloin steak, cut into strips

1 large red onion, sliced thickly

2 cloves garlic, crushed

½-inch piece fresh ginger, grated

1 teaspoon five-spice powder

8 ounces fresh shiitake mushrooms,
  sliced thickly

1 large red bell pepper, sliced thinly

½ cup hoisin sauce

1 ½ tablespoons soy sauce

1 ½ tablespoons rice wine vinegar

1 Heat 1 ½ tablespoons of the oil in wok; stir-fry cabbage and chives until cabbage is wilted. Remove from wok; cover to keep warm.

2 Heat 1 ½ tablespoons of the remaining oil in same wok; stir-fry beef, in batches, until browned.

3 Heat remaining oil in same wok; stir-fry onion until soft. Add garlic, ginger, five-spice, mushrooms and bell pepper; stir-fry until vegetables are tender. Return beef to wok with sauces and vinegar; stir-fry until heated through. Serve with cabbage mixture.

NUTRITIONAL INFO PER SERVING 23g total fat (6g saturated fat); 28g carbohydrate; 46g protein; 8g fiber; 498 calories

beef and mushroom stir fry

preparation time 15 minutes **cooking time** 15 minutes **serves** 4

You can find kecap manis in Asian or Indian markets, or you can make your own by heating equal parts soy sauce and brown sugar or molasses, stirring until sugar or molasses is dissolved.

¼ cup peanut oil

1 ¾ pounds rump roast or sirloin steak, sliced thinly

1 medium onion, sliced thickly

2 cloves garlic, crushed

¾-inch piece fresh ginger, grated

1 Thai chili, sliced thinly

5 ounces oyster mushrooms, halved

3 ½ ounces fresh shiitake mushrooms, halved

3 ½ ounces cremini mushrooms

1 pound Asian noodles

6 green onions, sliced thickly

¼ cup oyster sauce

1 ½ tablespoons kecap manis

1 teaspoon sesame oil

1 Heat half of the peanut oil in wok; stir-fry beef, in batches, until browned.

2 Heat remaining peanut oil in same wok; stir-fry onions until soft. Add garlic, ginger, chili and mushrooms; stir-fry until mushrooms are just tender.

3 Place noodles in large heatproof bowl, cover with boiling water, separate with fork; drain.

4 Return beef to wok with noodles and remaining ingredients; stir-fry until mixture boils and thickens slightly.

NUTRITIONAL INFO PER SERVING 30g total fat (9g saturated fat); 70g carbohydrate; 59g protein; 7g fiber; 789 calories

black bean, beef and asparagus stir-fry

preparation time 10 minutes **cooking time** 15 minutes **serves** 4

Look for salted dried black beans in Asian markets.

1 ½ tablespoons rice vinegar

1 ½ tablespoons soy sauce

1 ½ tablespoons dry sherry

2 cloves garlic, crushed

1 ¾ pounds sirloin steak, cut into strips

3 tablespoons peanut oil

3 tablespoons salted dried black beans

2 medium onions, sliced thickly

1 pound asparagus, trimmed, halved

1 teaspoon cornstarch

3 tablespoons oyster sauce

⅓ cup beef stock

1 Combine vinegar, soy sauce, sherry and garlic in large bowl, add beef; toss beef to coat in mixture.

2 Heat half of the oil in wok; stir-fry beef, in batches, until browned.

3 Rinse beans; drain, mash with fork in small bowl. Heat remaining oil in same wok; stir-fry beans, onion and asparagus until onion just softens. Return beef to wok with blended cornstarch, oyster sauce and stock; stir-fry until mixture boils and thickens slightly.

NUTRITIONAL INFO PER SERVING 16g total fat (5g saturated fat); 7g carbohydrate; 44g protein; 2g fiber; 359 calories

Chinese ground beef and spicy green beans

preparation time 10 minutes **cooking time** 15 minutes **serves** 4

1 ½ tablespoons peanut oil

1 ¾ pounds ground beef

2 cloves garlic, crushed

1 ¼-inch piece fresh ginger, grated

1 jalapeño pepper, sliced thinly lengthwise

10 ½ ounces green beans,
   halved lengthwise

1 medium onion, sliced thinly

1 ½ tablespoons fresh lime juice

3 tablespoons light soy sauce

1 ½ tablespoons white sugar

⅓ cup crushed roasted unsalted peanuts

1 Heat half the oil in wok; stir-fry beef, in batches, until browned and cooked.

2 Heat remaining oil in wok; stir-fry garlic, ginger, jalapeño, beans and onion until beans are almost tender.

3 Return beef to wok with lime juice, soy sauce and sugar; stir-fry until hot. Sprinkle with nuts, and serve.

NUTRITIONAL INFO PER SERVING 24g total fat (7g saturated fat); 10g carbohydrate; 46g protein; 4g fiber; 446 calories

twice-fried Szechwan beef

preparation time 20 minutes   **cooking time** 25 minutes   **serves** 4

1 ¼-pound piece beef tenderloin,
    sliced thinly
3 tablespoons dry sherry
3 tablespoons low-sodium soy sauce
1 teaspoon brown sugar
½ cup cornstarch
1 ½ cups jasmine rice
vegetable oil, for deep-frying
2 teaspoons sesame oil
1 clove garlic, crushed
1 fresh red serrano or Thai chili,
    chopped finely
1 medium onion, sliced thickly
2 medium carrots, halved, sliced thinly
1 small red bell pepper, sliced thinly
1 pound Chinese broccoli,
    chopped coarsely
1 ½ tablespoons cracked Szechwan
    peppercorns
3 tablespoons oyster sauce
¼ cup low-sodium soy sauce
½ cup beef stock
2 teaspoons brown sugar

1   Combine beef, sherry, 3 tablespoons of soy sauce and 1 teaspoon brown sugar in medium bowl. Let stand 10 minutes; drain. Toss beef mixture in cornstarch; shake off excess.

2   Cook rice in large pot of boiling water, uncovered, until just tender; drain. Cover to keep warm.

3   Heat vegetable oil in wok or large pot; deep-fry beef, in batches, until crisp. Drain on paper towels. Reserve oil for another use.

4   Heat sesame oil in same cleaned wok; stir-fry garlic, chili and onion until onion softens. Add carrots and bell pepper; stir-fry until just tender. Add Chinese broccoli; stir-fry until just wilted. Add beef with peppercorns, oyster sauce, ¼ cup soy sauce, stock and 2 teaspoons of brown sugar; stir-fry until heated through. Serve with rice.

Tip   It is easier to slice beef thinly if it is partially frozen.

NUTRITIONAL INFO PER SERVING 17g total fat (4g saturated fat); 94g carbohydrate; 42g protein; 6g fiber; 725 calories

breaded veal cutlets with gnocchi in garlic mushroom sauce

preparation time 15 minutes **cooking time** 35 minutes **serves** 4

2 eggs, beaten lightly

3 tablespoons milk

¼ cup all-purpose flour

¾ cup dried breadcrumbs

¾ cup coarse breadcrumbs

¾ cup mozzarella cheese

½ cup coarsely chopped fresh
flat-leaf parsley

8 veal cutlets (2 pounds)

¼ cup olive oil

2 cloves garlic, sliced thinly

8 ounces mushrooms, sliced thinly

¾ cup heavy cream

½ cup beef stock

1 ¼ pounds potato gnocchi

1 Whisk eggs, milk and flour in medium bowl. Combine breadcrumbs, cheese and ⅓ cup of the parsley in another medium bowl. Coat cutlets, one at a time, in egg mixture then in cheese mixture. Place cutlets, in single layer, on baking sheet. Cover; refrigerate 10 minutes.

2 Heat half of the oil in large skillet; cook cutlets, in batches, until browned on both sides and cooked to degree of desired doneness. Cover to keep warm.

3 Heat remaining oil in same skillet; cook garlic and mushrooms, stirring, until mushrooms are just tender. Add heavy cream and stock; bring to a boil. Reduce heat; simmer, stirring, until sauce thickens slightly.

4 Cook gnocchi in large pot of boiling water, uncovered, until gnocchi float to the surface. Remove from pot with slotted spoon; place in large bowl.

5 Stir remaining parsley into sauce; pour sauce over gnocchi, toss to combine. Serve gnocchi with cutlets.

NUTRITIONAL INFO PER SERVING 46g total fat (20g saturated fat); 75g carbohydrate; 70g protein; 7g fiber; 1009 calories

saltimbocca with risotto Milanese

preparation time 10 minutes **cooking time** 25 minutes **serves** 4

Saltimbocca is a classic Italian veal dish that literally means "jump in the mouth."

8 veal cutlets (1 ½ pounds)

4 slices prosciutto (2 ounces), halved crosswise

8 fresh sage leaves

½ cup finely grated pecorino romano cheese

3 tablespoons butter

1 cup dry white wine

1 ½ tablespoons coarsely chopped fresh sage

Risotto Milanese

1 ½ cups water

2 cups chicken stock

½ cup dry white wine

¼ teaspoon saffron threads

1 ½ tablespoons butter

1 large onion, chopped finely

2 cups arborio rice

¼ cup finely grated parmesan cheese

1 Place cutlets on cutting board. Place one piece prosciutto, one sage leaf and one-eighth of the cheese on each steak; fold in half to secure filling, secure with a toothpick or small skewer.

2 Make risotto Milanese.

3 Melt half of the butter in medium non-stick skillet; cook saltimbocca, in batches, 5 minutes or until browned on both sides and cooked through. Cover to keep warm.

4 Pour wine into same skillet; bring to a boil. Boil, uncovered, until wine reduces by half. Stir in remaining butter and chopped sage.

5 Divide risotto and saltimbocca among serving plates; drizzle saltimbocca with sauce.

Risotto Milanese Place the water, stock, wine and saffron in medium pot; bring to a boil. Reduce heat; simmer, covered. Heat butter in skillet; cook onion, stirring, until softened. Add rice; stir to coat rice in onion mixture. Stir in ½ cup of the simmering stock mixture; cook, stirring, over low heat, until liquid is absorbed. Continue adding stock mixture, ½ cup at a time, stirring until absorbed after each addition. Total cooking time should be about 35 minutes or until rice is just tender. Stir cheese gently into risotto.

NUTRITIONAL INFO PER SERVING 23g total fat (13g saturated fat); 83g carbohydrate; 54g protein; 2g fiber; 824 calories

veal cutlets with white bean salad

preparation time 15 minutes **cooking time** 10 minutes **serves** 4

1 ½ tablespoons olive oil

8 veal cutlets (1 ½ pounds)

½ cup beef stock

5 tablespoons butter

White bean salad

3 ½ cups baby arugula

1 large tomato, chopped coarsely

½ cup firmly packed fresh basil, torn

two 14 ½-ounce cans cannellini or
   Great Northern beans, rinsed, drained

1 ½ tablespoons finely chopped
   fresh chives

¼ cup fresh lemon juice

2 cloves garlic, crushed

¼ cup olive oil

1 Make white bean salad.

2 Heat oil in large non-stick skillet; cook cutlets, in batches, until browned on both sides and cooked to desired degree of doneness. Cover to keep warm.

3 Pour stock into same skillet; bring to a boil, stirring. Add butter, stir until butter melts. Reduce heat; simmer, stirring, 2 minutes.

4 Serve cutlets, drizzled with sauce, accompanied by white bean salad.

White bean salad Place arugula, tomato, basil and beans in large bowl. Whisk together chives, lemon juice, garlic and oil. Pour dressing over salad; toss gently to combine.

NUTRITIONAL INFO PER SERVING 39g total fat (13g saturated fat); 6g carbohydrate; 42g protein; 4g fiber; 541 calories

wiener schnitzel with lemon spaetzle

preparation time 20 minutes (plus refrigeration time) **cooking time** 20 minutes **serves** 4

Spaetzle are tiny dumplings made by pushing a batter through the holes of a colander or strainer into a pot of boiling water.

½ cup all-purpose flour
3 eggs, beaten lightly
3 tablespoons milk
2 cups coarse breadcrumbs
¾ cup dried breadcrumbs
½ cup finely grated parmesan cheese
8 veal cutlets (1 ¾ pounds)
vegetable oil, for shallow-frying

Lemon spaetzle
2 cups all-purpose flour
4 eggs, beaten lightly
½ cup water
2 teaspoons finely grated lemon peel
3 tablespoons butter, chopped

1 Whisk flour, eggs and milk in medium shallow bowl; combine breadcrumbs and cheese in another medium shallow bowl. Coat cutlets, one at a time, in flour mixture then in breadcrumb mixture. Place, in single layer, on baking sheet. Cover; refrigerate 15 minutes.

2 Make lemon spaetzle.

3 Heat oil in large skillet; cook cutlets, in batches, until browned on both sides and cooked through.

4 Serve schnitzel with lemon spaetzle.

Lemon spaetzle Place flour in large bowl, make well in center. Gradually add egg and the water, stirring, until batter is smooth. Stir in lemon peel. Pour half of the batter into metal colander set over large pot of boiling water; using wooden spoon, push batter through holes of colander, remove colander. When water returns to a boil, boil, uncovered, about 2 minutes or until spaetzle float to the surface. Use slotted spoon to remove spaetzle; drain, place in large bowl. Add half of the butter; toss spaetzle gently until butter melts. Keep warm; repeat with remaining batter and butter.

NUTRITIONAL INFO PER SERVING 43g total fat (14g saturated fat); 11g carbohydrate; 78g protein; 6g fiber; 1136 calories

veal scallopine with arugula and pistachio pesto

preparation time 10 minutes (plus refrigeration time) **cooking time** 15 minutes **serves** 4

1 ¼ pounds piece veal rump, sliced thinly

1 ½ tablespoons olive oil

¼ cup dry white wine

2 teaspoons finely grated lemon peel

1 clove garlic, crushed

12 ounces fettucine

Arugula and pistachio pesto

2 cups baby arugula, trimmed

½ cup shelled pistachios, roasted

⅓ cup coarsely grated parmesan cheese

1 clove garlic, quartered

1 ½ tablespoons fresh lemon juice

¾ cup olive oil

1 Combine veal, oil, wine, lemon peel and garlic in medium bowl; toss to coat veal in marinade. Cover; refrigerate.

2 Cook pasta in large pot of boiling salted water, uncovered, until just tender.

3 Cook veal, in batches, on heated oiled grill pan or skillet until browned all over and cooked to desired degree of doneness.

4 Combine drained pasta in large bowl with half of the pesto; toss gently to combine.

5 Serve veal on pasta topped with remaining pesto.

Arugula and pistachio pesto Blend or process arugula, nuts, cheese and garlic until well combined. With motor running, gradually add lemon juice and oil in thin stream until pesto thickens slightly.

Tip If possible, marinate the veal the night before serving so the flavors can penetrate the meat.

NUTRITIONAL INFO PER SERVING 59g total fat (9g saturated fat); 67g carbohydrate; 50g protein; 5g fiber; 1014 calories

veal with mushrooms and mustard cream sauce

preparation time 5 minutes **cooking time** 20 minutes **serves** 4

1 ½ tablespoons olive oil

8 veal cutlets (1 ¼ pounds)

1 tablespoon butter

1 clove garlic, crushed

5 ounces button mushrooms,
  sliced thickly

⅓ cup dry white wine

1 ½ tablespoons whole-grain mustard

½ cup heavy cream

¼ cup chicken stock

1 teaspoon fresh thyme leaves

1 Heat oil in large nonstick skillet; cook veal, in batches, until browned on both sides and cooked to desired degree of doneness. Cover to keep warm.

2 Melt butter in same skillet; cook garlic and mushrooms, stirring, until mushrooms just soften. Add wine and mustard; cook, stirring, 2 minutes. Add cream and stock; bring to a boil. Reduce heat; simmer, uncovered, about 5 minutes or until sauce thickens slightly. Stir in thyme.

3 Divide veal equally among serving plates; top with sauce. Serve with pasta.

NUTRITIONAL INFO PER SERVING 23g total fat (12g saturated fat); 1g carbohydrate; 40g protein; 1g fiber; 387 calories

marjoram and lemon-grilled veal chops with Greek salad

preparation time 25 minutes (plus refrigeration time) **cooking time** 10 minutes **serves** 4

1 teaspoon finely grated lemon peel

¼ cup fresh lemon juice

1 ½ tablespoons finely chopped
   fresh marjoram

2 teaspoons olive oil

four 7-ounce veal chops

Greek salad

¾ cup pitted Kalamata olives

7 ounces feta cheese, chopped coarsely

6 large plum tomatoes (about 1 pound),
   seeded, chopped coarsely

1 medium red bell pepper,
   chopped coarsely

2 small cucumbers, seeded, sliced thinly

2 celery stalks, sliced thinly

1 ½ tablespoons fresh marjoram

Lemon dressing

1 clove garlic, crushed

⅓ cup fresh lemon juice

2 teaspoons olive oil

1 Combine lemon peel, lemon juice, marjoram and oil in large bowl, add veal; toss veal to coat in marinade. Cover; refrigerate.

2 Make Greek salad and lemon dressing.

3 Cook veal on heated lightly oiled grill pan or skillet until cooked to desired degree of doneness.

4 Pour dressing over salad; toss gently to combine. Serve veal with salad.

Greek salad Combine ingredients in large bowl.

Lemon dressing Whisk together ingredients in small bowl.

Tip If possible, marinate the veal the night before serving so the flavors can penetrate the meat.

NUTRITIONAL INFO PER SERVING 20g total fat (9g saturated fat); 15g carbohydrate; 41g protein; 5g fiber; 405 calories

mustard-crusted rack of veal with mashed sweet potatoes

preparation time 25 minutes **cooking time** 35 minutes **serves** 4

3 tablespoons whole-grain mustard

3 green onions, chopped finely

2 cloves garlic, crushed

1 ½ tablespoons finely chopped
  fresh rosemary

3 tablespoons olive oil

2 pounds veal rack (8 cutlets), trimmed

2 small sweet potatoes (1 pound),
  chopped coarsely

1 ½ tablespoons butter

⅓ cup heavy cream

1 large onion, sliced thinly

14 ounces mushrooms, sliced thinly

1 ½ tablespoons all-purpose flour

¼ cup dry white wine

¾ cup chicken stock

¼ cup coarsely chopped fresh
  flat-leaf parsley

1 Preheat oven to 400°F.

2 Combine mustard, green onions, half of the garlic, rosemary and half of the oil in small measuring cup. Place veal on wire rack over large shallow baking dish; coat veal all over with mustard mixture. Roast, uncovered, about 30 minutes or until browned all over and cooked to desired degree of doneness. Cover to keep warm.

3 Boil, steam or microwave sweet potatoes until tender; drain. Mash sweet potatoes in large bowl with butter and half of the cream until smooth.

4 Heat remaining oil and pan juices in large skillet; cook onion and remaining garlic, stirring, until onion softens. Add mushrooms; cook, stirring, about 5 minutes or until just tender. Add flour; cook, stirring, until mixture thickens and bubbles. Gradually stir in wine and stock; stir until sauce boils and thickens. Add remaining cream and parsley; stir until heated through.

5 Serve veal with mashed sweet potatoes and mushroom sauce.

NUTRITIONAL INFO PER SERVING 27g total fat (11g saturated fat); 22g carbohydrate; 53g protein; 6g fiber; 567 calories

fennel-flavored veal chops with garlic mustard butter

preparation time 10 minutes **cooking time** 15 minutes **serves** 4

2 teaspoons fennel seeds

1 teaspoon sea salt or kosher salt

½ teaspoon cracked black pepper

2 tablespoons olive oil

four 6-ounce veal chops

4 portabello mushrooms

4 tablespoons butter, softened

1 tablespoon coarsely chopped
   fresh flat-leaf parsley

1 clove garlic, crushed

1 tablespoon whole-grain mustard

3 ounces baby arugula leaves

1 Using mortar and pestle, coarsely crush fennel seeds, salt, and pepper; stir in oil. Rub mixture all over veal.

2 Cook veal and mushrooms on grill pan or skillet until browned on both sides and cooked to desired degree of doneness.

3 Combine butter, parsley, garlic, and mustard in small bowl.

4 Divide arugula among serving plates, and top each with mushroom and veal; top with garlic mustard butter.

NUTRITIONAL INFO PER SERVING 30g total fat (13g saturated fat); 2g carbohydrate; 40g protein; 3g fiber; 438 calories

Pork

Pork is a perfect quick fix. It's lean and flavorful and pairs especially well with fruit and sweet marinades.

honey mustard pork chops with celeriac salad

preparation time 5 minutes   **cooking time** 15 minutes   **serves** 4

2 teaspoons honey

1 teaspoon Dijon mustard

1 ½ tablespoons olive oil

4 pork chops (2 pounds)

14 ounces baby carrots, trimmed

1¼ pounds celeriac, grated coarsely

⅓ cup mayonnaise

1 clove garlic, crushed

⅓ cup light sour cream

3 tablespoons fresh lemon juice

½ cup coarsely chopped fresh
   flat-leaf parsley

2 teaspoons Dijon mustard

1 Whisk honey, 1 teaspoon of mustard and oil in large bowl, add pork; toss pork to coat in mixture. Cook pork on heated oiled grill pan or skillet until cooked to desired degree of doneness. Cover pork; let stand 5 minutes.

2 Boil, steam or microwave carrots until just tender; drain. Cover to keep warm.

3 Combine celeriac, mayonnaise, garlic, sour cream, lemon juice, parsley and 2 teaspoons of mustard in medium bowl.

4 Serve chops with celeriac salad and carrots.

NUTRITIONAL INFO PER SERVING 38g total fat (10g saturated fat); 16g carbohydrate; 46g protein; 9g fiber; 584 calories

barbecued spareribs with red cabbage coleslaw

preparation time 15 minutes (plus refrigeration time) **cooking time** 25 minutes **serves** 4

4 ½-pound slab pork spareribs

Barbecue sauce

1 cup tomato sauce

¾ cup cider vinegar

3 tablespoons olive oil

¼ cup Worcestershire sauce

⅓ cup firmly packed brown sugar

3 tablespoons yellow mustard

1 teaspoon cracked black pepper

1-2 fresh small red serrano peppers,
chopped finely (optional)

2 cloves garlic, crushed

3 tablespoons fresh lemon juice

Red cabbage coleslaw

½ cup sour cream

¼ cup fresh lemon juice

3 tablespoons water

½ small red cabbage (1 ¼ pounds),
shredded finely

3 green onions, sliced thinly

1 Make barbecue sauce.

2 Place ribs in large shallow baking dish. Pour sauce over ribs, cover; refrigerate, turning ribs occasionally.

3 Make red cabbage coleslaw.

4 Drain ribs; reserve sauce. Cook ribs on heated oiled grill pan, brushing occasionally with reserved sauce, about 15 minutes or until cooked. Turn ribs midway through cooking time.

5 Bring remaining sauce to a boil in small pot; cook about 4 minutes or until sauce thickens slightly.

6 Cut ribs into serving-sized pieces; serve with hot barbecue sauce and coleslaw.

Barbecue sauce Combine ingredients in medium pot; bring to a boil. Cool 10 minutes.

Red cabbage coleslaw Whisk together sour cream, lemon juice and water. Place cabbage and onion in large bowl with dressing; toss gently to combine. Cover; refrigerate until needed.

Tip If possible, marinate the ribs the night before serving so the flavors can penetrate the meat.

NUTRITIONAL INFO PER SERVING 40g total fat (15g saturated fat); 44g carbohydrate; 54g protein; 8g fiber; 768 calories

marmalade-glazed pork chops

preparation time 5 minutes   **cooking time** 20 minutes   **serves** 4

½ cup dry red wine

⅓ cup orange marmalade

1 clove garlic, crushed

⅓ cup fresh orange juice

1 ½ tablespoons olive oil

4 pork chops (2 pounds)

1 Combine wine, marmalade, garlic and orange juice in small pot; bring to a boil. Remove from heat.

2 Heat oil in large skillet; cook pork until browned on both sides and cooked to desired degree of doneness, brushing constantly with marmalade glaze.

3 Serve pork chops with steamed rice and stir-fried baby bok choy or broccoli rabe, if desired.

NUTRITIONAL INFO PER SERVING 21g total fat (6g saturated fat); 20g carbohydrate; 28g protein; 1g fiber; 465 calories

roast pork with mustard and caramelized apples

preparation time 10 minutes **cooking time** 25 minutes **serves** 4

1 medium red onion, cut into thin wedges

1 ½ tablespoons olive oil

1 ¾ pounds pork tenderloin

½ cup honey Dijon whole-grain mustard

½ cup apple juice

⅓ cup vegetable or chicken stock

¼ cup coarsely chopped fresh
  flat-leaf parsley

4 tablespoons butter

4 large apples (about 1 ¾ pounds),
  peeled, cored, sliced thinly

3 tablespoons brown sugar

1 Preheat oven to 475°F.

2 Combine onion and oil in large ovenproof skillet. Brush pork all over with mustard; place on onion in skillet. Bake, uncovered, in oven about 20 minutes or until cooked to desired degree of doneness. Remove pork from skillet, cover; let stand 5 minutes.

3 Place skillet over medium heat; add apple juice and stock, bring to a boil. Reduce heat; simmer, uncovered, about 3 minutes or until sauce thickens slightly. Stir in parsley.

4 Melt butter in large skillet. Add apples and sugar; cook, stirring occasionally, about 10 minutes or until almost caramelized. Cover to keep warm.

5 Slice pork thickly; serve with onion sauce and apples, accompanied by a watercress salad, if desired.

NUTRITIONAL INFO PER SERVING 23g total fat (10g saturated fat); 30g carbohydrate; 45g protein; 5g fiber; 511 calories

pork chops with goat cheese and beet salad

preparation time 20 minutes **cooking time** 45 minutes **serves** 4

10 ½ ounces baby beets

1 ½ tablespoons caraway seeds

2 teaspoons olive oil

four 6-ounce butterflied pork chops

5 ounces firm goat cheese, crumbled

5 large red radishes, trimmed, sliced thinly

4 cups baby arugula

Dijon vinaigrette

2 teaspoons Dijon mustard

2 teaspoons olive oil

3 tablespoons red wine vinegar

1 Preheat oven to 400°F.

2 Discard beet stems and leaves; place unpeeled beets in small shallow baking dish. Roast, uncovered, about 45 minutes or until beets are tender. Cool 10 minutes; peel, cut into quarters.

3 Make Dijon vinaigrette.

4 Using mortar and pestle, crush seeds and oil into smooth paste; rub onto pork. Cook pork on heated lightly oiled grill pan until cooked to desired degree of doneness.

5 Place beets and vinaigrette in large bowl with cheese, radishes and arugula; toss gently to combine. Serve pork with salad.

Dijon vinaigrette Whisk together ingredients in small bowl.

NUTRITIONAL INFO PER SERVING 24g total fat (9g saturated fat); 7g carbohydrate; 47g protein; 3g fiber; 431 calories

pork tenderloin with orange and fennel

preparation time 10 minutes (plus standing time) **cooking time** 35 minutes **serves** 8

3 pounds pork tenderloin

2 cloves garlic, sliced thinly lengthwise

16 small fresh sage leaves

1 teaspoon fennel seeds

3 tablespoons olive oil

1 medium onion, sliced

¾ cup chicken stock

¼ cup fresh orange juice

1 Cut a few small slits along the top of pork; push in garlic and sage. Sprinkle pork with fennel seeds; let stand 30 minutes.

2 Preheat oven to 425°F.

3 Heat half of the oil in large ovenproof skillet; cook pork until browned all over. Remove pork from skillet.

4 Heat remaining oil in same skillet; cook onion, stirring, until lightly browned. Return pork to skillet. Drizzle with stock and orange juice. Roast, uncovered, in oven about 10 minutes or until pork is cooked through. Let stand, covered, 10 minutes, before slicing and serving with seasoned pan juices.

NUTRITIONAL INFO PER SERVING 20g total fat (6g saturated fat); 2g carbohydrate; 40g protein; 1g fiber; 346 calories

pork tacos with corn salsa

preparation time 15 minutes **cooking time** 15 minutes **serves** 4

3 tablespoons vegetable oil

1-ounce packet taco seasoning mix

1 ¼ pounds boneless pork chops,
  sliced thinly

16 corn tortillas

1 head Boston lettuce, torn

½ cup light sour cream

Corn salsa

10 ½ ounces canned corn, drained

3 medium tomatoes (about 1 pound),
  chopped coarsely

1 small red onion, chopped finely

½ cup coarsely chopped fresh cilantro

1 Combine oil and seasoning in medium bowl, add pork; toss pork to coat in mixture. Cook pork in large heated non-stick skillet until cooked to desired degree of doneness.

2 Wrap tortillas in foil. Heat in hot skillet about 5 minutes, turning occasionally, until warm.

3 Make Corn salsa.

4 Divide pork, salsa and remaining ingredients among tortillas; roll to enclose filling.

Corn salsa Combine ingredients in medium bowl.

NUTRITIONAL INFO PER SERVING 25g total fat (9g saturated fat); 46g carbohydrate; 42g protein; 8g fiber; 573 calories

Mexican spiced pork with avocado salsa

preparation time 10 minutes **cooking time** 10 minutes **serves** 4

3 tablespoons taco seasoning mix

¼ cup olive oil

four 8-ounce pork chops

3 small tomatoes, seeded, chopped finely

1 small avocado, chopped finely

1 cucumber, seeded, chopped finely

1 ½ tablespoons fresh lime juice

1 Combine seasoning, 3 tablespoons of the oil and pork in large bowl. Cook pork on heated oiled grill pan or skillet until cooked to desired degree of doneness.

2 Combine remaining oil in medium bowl with tomatoes, avocado, cucumber and lime juice. Serve pork with salsa.

NUTRITIONAL INFO PER SERVING 42g total fat (11g saturated fat); 1g carbohydrate; 38g protein; 1g fiber; 536 calories

sticky pork with veggies

preparation time 15 minutes (plus refrigeration time) **cooking time** 25 minutes **serves** 4

1 ½ tablespoons honey

3 tablespoons light soy sauce

3 tablespoons brown sugar

1 teaspoon five-spice powder

1 teaspoon chili powder

3 cloves garlic, crushed

1 teaspoon sesame oil

1 ¾ pounds pork loin chops,
   cut into 1 ¼-inch pieces

3 tablespoons peanut oil

½ cup raw peanuts, chopped coarsely

2 medium carrots, cut into matchsticks

5 ounces snow peas, trimmed,
   sliced thinly lengthwise

3 tablespoons fresh orange juice

3 strips fresh lime peel, chopped finely

4 green onions, sliced thinly

1 Combine honey, soy sauce, sugar, five-spice, chili powder, garlic and sesame oil in large bowl; add pork, turn to coat in marinade. Cover; refrigerate.

2 Heat half of the peanut oil in wok; stir-fry nuts until browned. Drain.

3 Heat remaining peanut oil in wok; stir-fry pork, in batches, until browned. Return pork to wok with carrots; stir-fry until pork is cooked.

4 Add snow peas, orange juice and lime peel; stir-fry until snow peas are tender. Remove from heat; toss in onions and nuts.

Tip If possible, marinate the pork the night before using so the flavors can penetrate the meat.

NUTRITIONAL INFO PER SERVING 34g total fat (8g saturated fat); 19g carbohydrate; 46g protein; 4g fiber; 566 calories

pork and peapods

preparation time 15 minutes   **cooking time** 15 minutes   **serves** 6

3 tablespoons peanut oil

2 pounds boneless pork chops,
  sliced thinly

1 medium onion, chopped coarsely

2 cloves garlic, crushed

1 serrano or jalapeño pepper,
  chopped finely

8 ounces sugar snap peas, trimmed

¼ cup light soy sauce

⅓ cup sweet sherry

2 teaspoons finely grated orange peel

3 tablespoons fresh orange juice

1 teaspoon cornstarch

1 Heat half of the oil in wok; stir-fry pork, in batches, until browned.

2 Heat remaining oil in wok; stir-fry onion, garlic and pepper until onion softens. Add peas; stir-fry until peas are just tender.

3 Return pork to wok with soy sauce, sherry, orange peel and blended orange juice and cornstarch; stir-fry until sauce thickens slightly.

NUTRITIONAL INFO PER SERVING 10g total fat (2g saturated fat); 6g carbohydrate; 39g protein; 2g fiber; 286 calories

curried fried rice with pork and shrimp

preparation time 20 minutes **cooking time** 25 minutes **serves** 4

1 ¾ pounds boneless pork chops,
  sliced thinly
1 ½ tablespoons white sugar
3 tablespoons light soy sauce
4 ounces uncooked small shrimp
3 tablespoons peanut oil
2 eggs, beaten lightly
1 teaspoon curry powder
2 cloves garlic, crushed
2 cups cold cooked white long-grain rice
4 green onions, sliced thinly
2 cups frozen peas and corn

1 Combine pork in medium bowl with sugar and half the sauce. Peel and devein shrimp, leaving tails intact.

2 Heat 1 teaspoon of the oil in wok. Pour egg into wok; cook over medium heat, tilting wok, until almost set. Remove omelet from wok; roll tightly, slice thinly.

3 Heat 2 teaspoons of the remaining oil in wok; stir-fry pork, in batches, until cooked to desired degree of doneness.

4 Heat 1 teaspoon of remaining oil in wok; stir-fry shrimp until just changed in color. Remove from wok.

5 Heat remaining oil in wok; cook curry powder and garlic, stirring, until fragrant. Add rice, onions, peas and corn mixture and remaining sauce; stir-fry until vegetables are just tender.

6 Return pork, shrimp and half of the omelet to wok; stir-fry until heated through. Sprinkle fried rice with remaining omelet.

NUTRITIONAL INFO PER SERVING 18g total fat (4g saturated fat); 38g carbohydrate; 58g protein; 5g fiber; 559 calories

pork and noodle stir fry

preparation time 20 minutes **cooking time** 10 minutes **serves** 4

1 ¼ pounds Asian stir-fry noodles

1 ½ tablespoons cornstarch

½ cup water

¼ cup kecap manis

¼ cup hoisin sauce

3 tablespoons rice vinegar

3 tablespoons peanut oil

1 ¼ pounds pork loin chops, sliced thinly

1 medium onion, sliced thickly

2 cloves garlic, crushed

1 teaspoon grated fresh ginger

5 ounces sugar snap peas, trimmed

1 medium red bell pepper, sliced thinly

1 medium yellow bell pepper, sliced thinly

7 ounces baby bok choy, quartered

1 Place noodles in large heatproof bowl, cover with boiling water. Separate noodles with fork; drain.

2 Blend cornstarch with the water in small bowl; stir in sauces and vinegar.

3 Heat half of the oil in wok; stir-fry pork, in batches, until browned all over.

4 Heat remaining oil in wok; stir-fry onion, garlic and ginger until onion softens. Add peas, bell peppers and bok choy; stir-fry until vegetables are just tender.

5 Return pork to wok with noodles and sauce mixture; stir-fry until sauce thickens slightly.

Tip Make your own kecap manis by heating equal parts soy sauce and brown sugar or molasses, stirring until sugar or molasses dissolves.

NUTRITIONAL INFO PER SERVING 14g total fat (3g saturated fat); 53g carbohydrate; 44g protein; 8g fiber; 532 calories

quick pork fried rice

preparation time 20 minutes **cooking time** 15 minutes **serves** 4

1 ¼ pounds boneless pork chops,
  sliced thinly

1 ½ tablespoons honey

3 tablespoons kecap manis

2 teaspoons peanut oil

2 eggs, beaten lightly

2 medium carrots, cut into matchsticks

1 medium red bell pepper, sliced thinly

3 cups cold cooked white long-grain rice

8 green onions, sliced thinly

1 cup bean sprouts

3 tablespoons soy sauce

3 tablespoons Chinese barbecue sauce

1 Combine pork in medium bowl with honey and keçap manis.

2 Heat half the oil in wok. Pour eggs into wok; cook over medium heat, tilting pan, until almost set. Remove omelet from wok; roll tightly, slice thinly.

3 Heat remaining oil in wok; stir-fry pork, in batches, until cooked.

4 Stir-fry carrots and bell pepper in wok until just tender.

5 Return half the omelet to wok with rice, pork, onions, sprouts and sauces; stir-fry until hot. Remove from heat; sprinkle with remaining omelet.

Tip Make your own kecap manis by heating equal parts soy sauce and brown sugar or molasses, stirring until sugar or molasses dissolves.

NUTRITIONAL INFO PER SERVING 9g total fat (3g saturated fat); 55g carbohydrate; 43g protein; 5g fiber; 486 calories

pork with sweet and sour peaches

preparation time 20 minutes **cooking time** 10 minutes **serves** 4

3 tablespoons cornstarch

1 ¾ pounds pork loin, sliced thinly

3 tablespoons peanut oil

1 medium red onion, chopped coarsely

1 medium red bell pepper,
   cut into thin strips

1 medium yellow bell pepper,
   cut into thin strips

⅓ cup water

2 cloves garlic, crushed

3 tablespoons sugar

3 tablespoons white wine vinegar

3 tablespoons tomato sauce

3 tablespoons soy sauce

2 large peaches (about 1 pound),
   cut into wedges

⅓ cup coarsely chopped fresh cilantro

1 Rub cornstarch into pork in medium bowl.

2 Heat half of the oil in wok; stir-fry pork, in batches, until browned.

3 Heat remaining oil in same wok; stir-fry onion and bell peppers until tender.

4 Return pork to wok with the water, garlic, sugar, vinegar and sauces;
stir-fry until pork is cooked. Add peaches; stir-fry until hot. Remove from heat;
toss in cilantro.

NUTRITIONAL INFO PER SERVING 25g total fat (7g saturated fat);
27g carbohydrate; 46g protein; 3g fiber; 527 calories

teriyaki pork with pineapple

preparation time 20 minutes (plus refrigeration time) **cooking time** 20 minutes **serves** 4

⅓ cup mirin or dry white wine

¼ cup soy sauce

3 tablespoons cooking sake

2 teaspoons white sugar

2-inch piece fresh ginger, grated

2 cloves garlic, crushed

1 ¼ pounds boneless pork chops

1 small pineapple (2 pounds), sliced thinly

2 green onions, sliced thinly

1 Combine mirin, soy sauce, sake, sugar, ginger and garlic in large bowl; add pork, turn to coat in marinade. Cover; refrigerate 3 hours or overnight.

2 Drain pork; reserve marinade. Cook pork on heated oiled grill pan or skillet until browned and cooked to desired degree of doneness. Cover; let stand 10 minutes.

3 Cook pineapple on grill pan or skillet about 2 minutes or until soft.

4 Bring reserved marinade to a boil in small pot; cook about 5 minutes or until sauce reduces by half.

5 Serve sliced pork with pineapple and onions; drizzle with sauce.

NUTRITIONAL INFO PER SERVING 12g total fat (4g saturated fat); 13g carbohydrate; 34g protein; 3g fiber; 328 calories

jerk-spiced pork loin with butternut squash fries

preparation time 15 minutes **cooking time** 25 minutes **serves** 4

Piri piri, a Portuguese hot sauce, is made from a tiny red chili of the same name, ground with ginger, garlic, oil and various herbs. If you can't find it, substitute your favorite hot pepper sauce.

1-3 jalapeño peppers, chopped coarsely

3 green onions, chopped coarsely

2 cloves garlic, crushed

1 teaspoon ground allspice

1 teaspoon dried thyme

1 teaspoon sugar

1 ½ tablespoons soy sauce

1 ½ tablespoons fresh lime juice

four 9-ounce pork loin chops

2-pound piece butternut squash, trimmed

3 tablespoons vegetable oil

Piri piri dipping sauce

⅓ cup mayonnaise

3 tablespoons piri piri hot sauce

1 Combine chilies, onions, garlic, allspice, thyme, sugar, sauce, lime juice and pork in medium bowl.

2 Make piri piri dipping sauce.

3 Cut butternut squash into 3-inch strips; boil, steam or microwave until tender. Drain; combine strips with oil in medium bowl. Cook strips on heated oiled grill pan or skillet until browned.

4 Cook pork on heated oiled grill pan until cooked to desired degree of doneness. Serve pork with fries and dipping sauce.

Piri piri dipping sauce Combine ingredients in small bowl.

NUTRITIONAL INFO PER SERVING 39g total fat (10g saturated fat); 22g carbohydrate; 42g protein; 4g fiber; 611 calories

pork and lemongrass stir fry

preparation time 10 minutes **cooking time** 15 minutes **serves** 4

1 ½ tablespoons peanut oil

4-inch stick finely chopped fresh
    lemongrass

2 fresh small red serrano or Thai chilies,
    chopped finely (optional)

2 teaspoons finely grated fresh ginger

2 cloves garlic, crushed

1 pound ground pork

1 ½ tablespoons red curry paste

3 ½ ounces green beans, chopped coarsely

3 tablespoons fish sauce

3 tablespoons fresh lime juice

1 ½ tablespoons brown sugar

1 small red onion, sliced thinly

2 green onions, sliced thinly

¼ cup loosely packed fresh basil

¼ cup firmly packed fresh cilantro

¼ cup roasted peanuts, chopped coarsely

4 large iceberg lettuce leaves

1 Heat oil in wok or skillet; stir-fry lemongrass, chilies, ginger and garlic until fragrant. Add pork; stir-fry about 5 minutes or until pork changes color. Add curry paste; cook, stirring, until fragrant.

2 Add beans, fish sauce, lime juice and sugar to pan; stir-fry about 5 minutes or until beans are just tender. Remove from heat; stir in onions, basil, cilantro and half of the nuts.

3 Divide lettuce leaves among serving plates; spoon pork mixture into lettuce leaves, sprinkle with remaining nuts.

NUTRITIONAL INFO PER SERVING 20g total fat (5g saturated fat); 7g carbohydrate; 30g protein; 4g fiber; 323 calories

pork larb with broccolini

preparation time 15 minutes **cooking time** 10 minutes **serves** 4

Larb is a common Thai dish made with ground meat, lime juice and fish sauce.

1 tablespoon peanut oil

2 cloves garlic, crushed

1 ¼ pounds ground pork

⅓ cup brown sugar

2 tablespoons fish sauce

1 tablespoon grated lime peel

½ cup canned fried onions

⅓ cup roasted unsalted peanuts

¾ pound broccolini, trimmed and
   halved lengthwise

1 tablespoon fresh lime juice

1 cup loosely packed fresh cilantro leaves

1 red serrano pepper, sliced thinly
   (optional)

2 tablespoons coarsely chopped
   roasted unsalted peanuts

1 Heat oil in wok or skillet; stir-fry garlic and pork until pork is browned through. Remove with slotted spoon.

2 Add sugar, fish sauce, lime peel, fried onions, and whole peanuts to pan; bring to a boil. Reduce heat; simmer, uncovered, 1 minute. Return pork to pan; cook, uncovered, about 2 minutes or until mixture is slightly dry and sticky.

3 Boil, steam or microwave broccolini; drain.

4 Stir juice and ¾ cup of the cilantro into larb mixture off the heat; serve tossed with broccolini and sprinkled with remaining cilantro, serrano, and coarsely chopped nuts.

NUTRITIONAL INFO PER SERVING 24g total fat (6g saturated fat); 25g carbohydrate; 40g protein; 6g fiber; 480 calories

stir-fried pork with bok choy and rice noodles

preparation time 10 minutes **cooking time** 10 minutes **serves** 4

¼ cup oyster sauce

2 tablespoons soy sauce

2 tablespoons sweet sherry

1 tablespoon brown sugar

1 clove garlic, crushed

1 star anise, crushed

pinch Chinese five spice powder

12 ounces fresh rice noodles

2 teaspoons sesame oil

1 ¼ pounds pork loin, sliced thinly

1 ½ pounds baby bok choy,
chopped coarsely

1 Combine oyster sauce, soy sauce, sherry, sugar, garlic, star anise and five spice in small bowl.

2 Place noodles in large heatproof bowl, cover with boiling water; separate with fork, drain.

3 Heat oil in wok or skillet; stir-fry pork, in batches, until cooked to desired degree of doneness. Add sauce mixture, noodles and bok choy; stir-fry until bok choy is wilted.

Tip Rice noodles are more commonly found dried. Substitute 3 ounces dried noodles for this recipe.

NUTRITIONAL INFO PER SERVING 7g total fat (2g saturated fat); 32g carbohydrate; 38g protein; 3g fiber; 357 calories

Lamb

Mild and delicious, with a slightly buttery quality, lamb is often overlooked.
Slightly pink in the center is the way to go when roasting or pan-frying.
Leftover lamb, sliced thinly, makes a truly tasty sandwich.

honey and five-spice lamb with bok choy

preparation time 15 minutes **cooking time** 10 minutes **serves** 4

¼ teaspoon five spice powder

¼ cup oyster sauce

2 tablespoons honey

2 tablespoons rice vinegar

2 cloves garlic, crushed

1 ¼ pounds lamb fillets, sliced thinly

12 ounces fresh vermicelli rice noodles

1 tablespoon sesame oil

1-2 fresh jalapeño peppers, sliced thinly

1-inch piece fresh ginger, cut into
    matchsticks

1 medium red onion, cut into thick pieces

1 pound baby bok choy, leaves separated

¼ cup firmly packed fresh cilantro leaves

1 tablespoon crushed peanuts

1 Combine five spice, oyster sauce, honey, vinegar and garlic in small bowl.

2 Combine lamb with 1 tablespoon of the five spice mixture in medium bowl.

3 Place noodles in large heatproof bowl, and cover with boiling water; separate noodles with fork, and drain.

4 Stir-fry lamb in wok or skillet, in batches, until browned. Return lamb to pan; add remaining five spice mixture, jalapeño, ginger and onion; stir-fry until onion softens. Add noodles and bok choy; stir-fry until heated through.

5 Serve, sprinkled with cilantro and peanuts.

NUTRITIONAL INFO PER SERVING 12g total fat (3g saturated fat);
41g carbohydrate; 36g protein; 3g fiber; 426 calories

tamarind glazed rack of lamb with Asian greens and orange salad

preparation time 10 minutes **cooking time** 25 minutes **serves** 4

¼ cup tamarind concentrate

¼ cup orange juice

2 teaspoons sesame oil

1 ½ tablespoons brown sugar

2 Frenched lamb rib racks (1 ¼ pounds)

2 large oranges (about 1 ¼ pounds)

3 ½ ounces fresh tat soi, bok choy or
  spinach leaves

3 ½ ounces shiitake mushrooms,
  sliced thickly

1 Preheat oven to 400°F.

2 Combine tamarind, orange juice, oil and sugar in small pot; reserve 3 tablespoons of the mixture in large bowl. Bring remaining mixture in pot to a boil. Reduce heat; simmer, uncovered, about 2 minutes or until mixture thickens slightly.

3 Place lamb on metal rack inside large shallow baking dish; brush hot tamarind glaze over racks. Roast, uncovered, about 20 minutes or until racks are cooked to desired degree of doneness. Cover; let stand 10 minutes.

4 Segment oranges over reserved tamarind mixture in bowl. Add greens and mushrooms; toss gently to combine.

5 Cut each lamb rack in half; place two halves on each serving plate, serve with salad.

NUTRITIONAL INFO PER SERVING 15g total fat (6g saturated fat); 16g carbohydrate; 18g protein; 3g fiber; 271 calories

paprika dusted lamb loin with tomato feta salad

preparation time 15 minutes **cooking time** 10 minutes **serves** 4

8 lamb loin chops (1 ¾ pounds)

2 teaspoons sweet paprika

¼ cup olive oil

1 medium red bell pepper,
    chopped coarsely

1 medium green bell pepper,
    chopped coarsely

2 medium tomatoes, chopped coarsely

7 ounces feta cheese, cut into
    ¾-inch pieces

1 ½ tablespoons fresh lemon juice

¼ cup firmly packed fresh flat-leaf
    parsley leaves

1 Sprinkle chops with paprika. Heat 1 ½ tablespoons of the oil in large skillet; cook chops until browned on both sides and cooked to desired degree of doneness. Cover chops; let stand 5 minutes.

2 Combine bell peppers, tomatoes, cheese, lemon juice, parsley and remaining oil in large bowl; toss gently to combine.

3 Divide tomato feta salad and chops among serving plates; serve with lemon wedges, if desired.

NUTRITIONAL INFO PER SERVING 39g total fat (16g saturated fat); 4g carbohydrate; 43g protein; 2g fiber; 535 calories

Madras curry

preparation time 10 minutes **cooking time** 30 minutes **serves** 4

1 pound butternut squash, cut into
  ¾-inch pieces
7 ounces green beans, chopped coarsely
3 tablespoons vegetable oil
1 ¼ pounds lamb loin, cut into
  ¾-inch pieces
1 medium onion, chopped finely
2 cloves garlic, crushed
½ cup Madras curry paste
1 cup beef stock
14 ½-ounce can crushed tomatoes,
  drained
2 cups basmati rice
1 cup buttermilk
½ cup coarsely chopped fresh cilantro

1 Boil, steam or microwave squash and beans, separately, until just tender; drain. Rinse beans under cold water; drain.

2 Heat half of the oil in wok or skillet; stir-fry lamb, in batches, until just browned.

3 Heat remaining oil in same pan; stir-fry onion and garlic until onion softens. Add curry paste; stir-fry until fragrant. Return lamb to pan with stock and tomatoes; bring to a boil. Add squash, reduce heat; simmer curry, covered, stirring occasionally, 10 minutes.

4 Cook rice in large pot of boiling water, uncovered, until just tender; drain.

5 Add beans and buttermilk to curry; stir over low heat until heated through. Remove from heat; stir in cilantro. Serve curry with rice.

NUTRITIONAL INFO PER SERVING 37g total fat (10g saturated fat); 97g carbohydrate; 48g protein; 9g fiber; 916 calories

feta, spinach and prosciutto lamb rolls with herbed potatoes

preparation time 20 minutes **cooking time** 20 minutes **serves** 4

1 pound fingerling potatoes,
  halved lengthwise

1 ½ tablespoons butter

1 ½ tablespoons finely chopped
  fresh flat-leaf parsley

12 slices prosciutto (6 ounces)

1 cup baby spinach leaves

5 ½ ounces feta cheese, sliced thinly

four 7-ounce pieces lamb loin

1 ½ tablespoons olive oil

1 Boil, steam or microwave potatoes until tender; drain. Toss in large bowl with butter and parsley; cover to keep warm.

2 Slightly overlap three slices of the prosciutto, side by side, on board; layer with a quarter of the spinach, a quarter of the cheese and one piece of the lamb. Starting from narrow end of prosciutto slices, roll carefully to completely enclose lamb. Repeat with remaining prosciutto, spinach, cheese and lamb.

3 Heat oil in large skillet; cook lamb rolls about 15 minutes or until browned all over and cooked to desired degree of doneness. Cover lamb; let stand 10 minutes. Serve lamb sliced thickly with herbed potatoes.

NUTRITIONAL INFO PER SERVING 38g total fat (18g saturated fat); 17g carbohydrate; 60g protein; 3g fiber; 652 calories

spicy lamb with tabbouleh salad

preparation time 30 minutes (plus standing time) **cooking time** 10 minutes **serves** 4

1 clove garlic, crushed

1 teaspoon crushed red pepper flakes

1 ½ tablespoons sweet paprika

2 teaspoons ground coriander

1 teaspoon ground cumin

1 ½ tablespoons finely chopped fresh mint

3 tablespoons hot water

four 5-ounce lamb steaks

Tabbouleh salad

¼ cup bulgur wheat

2 ½ cups coarsely chopped fresh
    flat-leaf parsley

½ cup coarsely chopped fresh mint

½ cup coarsely chopped fresh cilantro

3 medium tomatoes (about 1 pound),
    seeded, chopped coarsely

1 medium red onion, chopped finely

⅔ cup fresh lemon juice

⅔ cup olive oil

1 Make tabbouleh salad.

2 Combine garlic, spices, mint and the water in medium bowl; add steaks, turn to coat in mixture. Cook lamb on heated oiled grill pan or skillet until browned on both sides and cooked to desired degree of doneness. Cover steaks; let stand 5 minutes.

3 Serve lamb with tabbouleh salad.

Tabbouleh salad Cover bulgur with cold water in small bowl; let stand about 10 minutes or until bulgur softens, drain well. Combine bulgar with herbs, tomatoes and onion in medium bowl. Whisk together lemon juice and oil, drizzle over tabbouleh; toss gently to combine.

Tip Herbs like mint, basil, and sage darken and become limp quickly once they've been chopped so try not to handle them until the last possible minute.

NUTRITIONAL INFO PER SERVING 44g total fat (8.4g saturated fat); 11.5g carbohydrate; 20.8g protein; 6.4g fiber; 525 calories

grilled lamb with fattoush salad

preparation time 25 minutes **cooking time** 10 minutes **serves** 4

Sumac is a dried berry grown in Italy and the Middle East, with a pleasantly fruity, astringent flavor.

1 clove garlic, crushed
1 teaspoon sweet paprika
1 ½ tablespoons sumac
1 teaspoon finely chopped fresh oregano
1 ½ tablespoons water
1 ½ tablespoons olive oil
1 ¾ pounds lamb loin

Fattoush salad
1 large pita
3 small cucumbers, seeded, chopped coarsely
3 medium tomatoes (about 1 pound), seeded, chopped coarsely
5 radishes, sliced thinly
3 green onions, sliced thickly
1 cup coarsely chopped fresh flat-leaf parsley
1 cup coarsely chopped fresh mint
1 head Romaine lettuce, torn
3 tablespoons sumac
⅓ cup fresh lemon juice
¼ cup olive oil

1 Combine garlic, paprika, sumac, oregano, the water and oil in medium bowl; add lamb, turn to coat in mixture.
2 Cook lamb on heated oiled grill pan or skillet until browned on both sides and cooked to desired degree of doneness. Cover lamb; let stand 10 minutes, slice thickly.
3 Make Fattoush salad.
4 Serve lamb with salad.
Fattoush salad Split pita in half; toast pita under preheated broiler. Combine cucumbers, tomatoes, radishes, onions, herbs and lettuce in large bowl. Whisk together sumac, lemon juice and oil, pour over salad; toss gently to combine. Break pita into small pieces over salad just before serving.

NUTRITIONAL INFO PER SERVING 37g total fat (11g saturated fat); 16g carbohydrate; 47g protein; 6g fiber; 583 calories

Mongolian lamb stir-fry

preparation time 15 minutes **cooking time** 20 minutes **serves** 4

1 ½ cups white long-grain rice

3 tablespoons peanut oil

1 ¼ pounds lamb, cut into strips

2 cloves garlic, crushed

½ inch piece fresh ginger, grated

1 medium onion, sliced thickly

1 medium red bell pepper, sliced thickly

8-ounce can bamboo shoots,
    rinsed, drained

¼ cup soy sauce

1 ½ tablespoons black bean sauce

1 ½ tablespoons cornstarch

3 tablespoons rice wine vinegar

6 green onions, cut into 2-inch lengths

1 Cook rice in large pot of boiling water, uncovered, until just tender; drain. Cover to keep warm.

2 Heat half of the oil in wok or skillet; stir-fry lamb, in batches, until browned all over.

3 Heat remaining oil in same pan; stir-fry garlic, ginger and onion until onion softens. Add bell pepper and bamboo shoots; stir-fry until vegetables are just tender. Return lamb to pan with sauces and blended cornstarch and vinegar; stir-fry until sauce boils and thickens slightly. Remove from heat; stir in green onions. Serve with rice.

NUTRITIONAL INFO PER SERVING 23g total fat (8g saturated fat); 69g carbohydrate; 40g protein; 4g fiber; 648 calories

rack of lamb with garlic and sage

preparation time 10 minutes **cooking time** 25 minutes **serves** 4

3 large red onions (about 2 pounds)

12 fresh sage leaves

⅓ cup olive oil

3 tablespoons coarsely chopped
   fresh sage

4 cloves garlic, chopped coarsely

four Frenched lamb racks (1 ¼ pounds)

1 Preheat oven to 425°F.

2 Halve onions, slice into thin wedges; place in bottom of a large baking dish with sage leaves and half of the oil.

3 Combine remaining oil in small bowl with chopped sage and garlic. Press sage mixture all over lamb; lay lamb on top of sliced onions.

4 Roast lamb, uncovered, about 25 minutes or until lamb is browned all over and cooked to desired degree of doneness. Cover lamb racks; let stand 10 minutes.

NUTRITIONAL INFO PER SERVING 31g total fat (9g saturated fat); 12g carbohydrate; 18g protein; 3g fiber; 401 calories

doner kebab

preparation time 25 minutes (plus refrigeration time) **cooking time** 10 minutes **serves** 4

Doner kebab is the origin of other similar Mediterranean and Middle Eastern dishes such as shawarma and gyros.

4 cloves garlic, crushed

1 teaspoon baharat spice

¼ cup olive oil

2 tablespoons fresh lemon juice

1 ¼ pounds lamb steaks or chops

2 cloves garlic, crushed

⅓ cup Greek-style yogurt

½ cup hummus

4 large pita breads

1 bunch watercress, shredded finely

3 large Roma tomatoes, seeded, chopped coarsely

1 Combine 4 cloves of garlic, baharat, 2 tablespoons of the oil, and 1 tablespoon of the lemon juice in large bowl; add lamb, turn to coat in mixture. Cover; refrigerate 3 hours or overnight.

2 Combine remaining oil and lemon juice, 2 cloves of garlic and yogurt in small bowl; cover and refrigerate until required.

3 Cook lamb on heated oiled grill pan or skillet until browned on both sides and cooked to desired degree of doneness. Slice thinly.

4 Spread hummus evenly over each pita; divide watercress, tomatoes, and lamb among pita; drizzle with yogurt sauce. Roll pita tightly to completely enclose filling.

Tip Baharat, a spice mix used in countries surrounding the Persian Gulf, can be made of any of an array of pungent spices, including paprika, chili, black pepper, cinnamon, clove, nutmeg, allspice, coriander, and cumin. Make a simple version by mixing 1 tablespoon black pepper, 1 tablespoon allspice, ½ teaspoon cinnamon and ¼ teaspoon nutmeg.

NUTRITIONAL INFO PER SERVING 36g total fat (11g saturated fat); 47g carbohydrate; 44g protein; 7g fiber; 690 calories

cardamom-crusted lamb chops with saffron spinach risotto

preparation time 15 minutes **cooking time** 40 minutes **serves** 4

¼ cup all-purpose flour

1 egg

1 cup dried breadcrumbs

1 teaspoon finely grated lemon peel

1 tablespoon ground cardamom

½ cup finely chopped fresh
   flat-leaf parsley

16 Frenched lamb chops (1 ¾ pounds)

3 cups chicken stock

2 cups water

6 tablespoons olive oil

1 clove garlic, crushed

1 medium yellow onion, chopped coarsely

1 ¼ cups arborio rice

pinch of saffron threads

¼ cup dry white wine

3 ounces baby spinach leaves

1 tablespoon butter

1 Place flour in small shallow bowl; whisk egg in separate small shallow bowl. Combine breadcrumbs, lemon peel, cardamom, and parsley in separate medium shallow bowl. Coat chops, one at a time, in flour then egg then breadcrumb mixture. Place chops, in single layer, on baking sheet; cover, and refrigerate until required.

2 Bring stock and the water to a boil in medium pot. Reduce heat; simmer, covered. Heat 2 tablespoons of the oil in large pot; cook garlic and onion, stirring, until onion softens. Add rice and saffron; stir rice to coat in mixture. Add wine; bring to a boil. Reduce heat; simmer, stirring, 2 minutes. Stir in 1 cup of the simmering stock mixture; cook, stirring, over low heat, until liquid is absorbed. Continue adding stock mixture, one cup at a time, stirring until liquid is absorbed after each addition. Total cooking time should be about 35 minutes or until rice is just tender. Stir spinach and butter into risotto just before serving.

3 When risotto is almost cooked, heat remaining oil in large skillet; cook chops, in batches, until browned on both sides and cooked to desired degree of doneness. Serve chops with risotto.

NUTRITIONAL INFO PER SERVING 47.2g total fat (14.7g saturated fat); 71g carbohydrate; 32.7g protein; 3.2g fiber; 846 calories

spicy lamb with fried noodles

preparation time 15 minutes **cooking time** 10 minutes **serves** 4

1 ¼ pounds Asian stir-fry noodles

1 ½ tablespoons Asian chili paste
(sambal oelek)

1 ½ tablespoons dark soy sauce

1 ½ tablespoons fish sauce

2 cloves garlic, crushed

1 ¾ pounds lamb loin, sliced thinly

¼ cup peanut oil

⅓ cup coarsely chopped brazil nuts

⅔ cup beef stock

3 tablespoons oyster sauce

3 tablespoons fresh lime juice

2 teaspoons brown sugar

5 ounces sugar snap peas, trimmed

⅓ cup finely chopped fresh mint

1-2 fresh small red serrano or jalapeño
peppers, chopped finely

1 Place noodles in large heatproof bowl, cover with boiling water; separate with fork, drain.

2 Combine chili paste, soy sauce, fish sauce and garlic in large bowl with lamb.

3 Heat ½ teaspoon of oil in wok or skillet; stir-fry nuts until browned lightly. Remove from pan.

4 Heat 3 tablespoons of the remaining oil in pan; stir-fry lamb, in batches, until browned.

5 Heat remaining oil in pan; stir-fry noodles until browned lightly.

6 Add stock, oyster sauce, lime juice and sugar to pan; simmer about 3 minutes or until sauce thickens slightly. Return lamb to pan with peas; stir-fry until hot.

7 Serve noodles topped with lamb mixture, sprinkled with nuts, mint and pepper.

NUTRITIONAL INFO PER SERVING 41g total fat (12g saturated fat);
45g carbohydrate; 50g protein; 5g fiber; 757 calories

lamb with white wine mascarpone sauce

preparation time 10 minutes **cooking time** 15 minutes **serves** 4

¼ cup olive oil

12 fresh sage leaves

3 ½ ounces sliced prosciutto

8 lamb chops (1 ¼ pounds)

1 clove garlic, crushed

¾ cup dry white wine

½ cup mascarpone cheese

¼ cup heavy cream

1 Heat oil in medium skillet; cook sage until crisp. Drain on paper towels. Cook prosciutto, stirring, until crisp; drain on paper towels.

2 Cook lamb in same skillet until browned on both sides and cooked to desired degree of doneness. Remove from skillet.

3 Cook garlic in same skillet, stirring, until fragrant. Add wine; bring to a boil. Reduce heat; simmer, uncovered, until liquid reduces by half. Add mascarpone and cream; cook, stirring, over medium heat until sauce boils and thickens slightly.

4 Divide lamb among serving plates; top with prosciutto and sage, drizzle with sauce. Serve with steamed asparagus.

NUTRITIONAL INFO PER SERVING 45g total fat (21g saturated fat); 1g carbohydrate; 38g protein; 1g fiber; 582 calories

iskander kebab

preparation time 15 minutes **cooking time** 15 minutes **serves** 4

Iskander kebab is a traditional Turkish dish made with lamb, but you can also try it with beef or chicken.

2 pounds boneless leg of lamb,
  cut into ¾-inch cubes
1 cup yogurt
3 tablespoons fresh lemon juice
2 cloves garlic, crushed
2 teaspoons finely chopped fresh thyme

Chili tomato sauce
1 ½ tablespoons olive oil
1 small onion, chopped coarsely
1 clove garlic, crushed
2 fresh poblano or anaheim peppers,
  seeded, chopped coarsely
2 medium tomatoes, chopped coarsely
1 ½ tablespoons tomato paste
⅓ cup dry red wine

1 Make chili tomato sauce.

2 Thread lamb onto skewers. Combine yogurt, lemon juice, garlic and thyme in small bowl. Reserve two-tirds of the yogurt mixture in a separate bowl. Use remaining yogurt mixture to brush lamb.

3 Cook lamb skewers, in batches, on heated oiled grill or grill pan until browned all over and cooked to desired degree of doneness.

4 Serve kebabs with reserved yogurt mixture and chili tomato sauce.

Chili tomato sauce Heat oil in medium skillet; cook onion and garlic, stirring, until onion softens. Add remaining ingredients; bring to a boil. Reduce heat; simmer, uncovered, about 5 minutes or until sauce thickens slightly. Blend or process sauce until smooth.

Tip Soak 8 bamboo skewers in cold water for an hour before using to prevent them from splintering and scorching.

NUTRITIONAL INFO PER SERVING 29g total fat (12g saturated fat); 7g carbohydrate; 57g protein; 2g fiber; 583 calories

grilled lamb with ratatouille

preparation time 20 minutes   **cooking time** 25 minutes   **serves** 4

5 baby eggplants, peeled,
   chopped coarsely

2 medium red bell peppers,
   chopped coarsely

1 medium yellow bell pepper,
   chopped coarsely

4 medium plum tomatoes (about 1 pound),
   chopped coarsely

1 medium onion, chopped coarsely

2 cloves garlic, sliced thickly

cooking-oil spray

four 5-ounce lamb steaks or chops

Balsamic dressing

1 ½ tablespoons olive oil

1 ½ tablespoons fresh lemon juice

1 ½ tablespoons balsamic vinegar

1 clove garlic, crushed

¼ cup loosely packed fresh oregano

1 Preheat oven to 425°F.

2 Make balsamic dressing.

3 Combine vegetables and garlic, in single layer, in two large shallow baking dishes; spray vegetables lightly with cooking-oil spray. Roast, uncovered, about 25 minutes or until ratatouille is just tender, stirring occasionally.

4 Cook lamb on heated oiled grill pan or skillet until cooked to desired degree of doneness.

5 Place ratatouille and half of the dressing in large bowl; toss gently to combine. Divide ratatouille and lamb among serving plates; drizzle with remaining dressing.

Balsamic dressing Whisk together ingredients in small bowl.

NUTRITIONAL INFO PER SERVING 13g total fat (5g saturated fat); 11g carbohydrate; 37g protein; 5g fiber; 313 calories

parmesan-breaded lamb chops

preparation time 15 minutes **cooking time** 15 minutes **serves** 4

⅓ cup all-purpose flour
12 Frenched lamb chops (2 pounds)
2 eggs
3 tablespoons milk
1 clove garlic, crushed
½ cup fresh breadcrumbs
½ cup dried breadcrumbs
½ cup finely grated parmesan cheese
1 ½ tablespoons finely chopped fresh oregano
3 tablespoons olive oil

1 Place flour in plastic bag. Add chops; toss to coat chops all over, shake off excess flour.
2 Combine eggs, milk and garlic in medium shallow bowl; combine breadcrumbs, cheese and oregano in another medium shallow bowl. Dip chops, one at a time, into egg mixture, then breadcrumb mixture.
3 Heat oil in large nonstick skillet; cook chops, in batches, until browned on both sides and cooked to desired degree of doneness. Serve sprinkled with fresh whole oregano leaves.

NUTRITIONAL INFO PER SERVING 27g total fat (10g saturated fat); 24g carbohydrate; 37g protein; 2g fiber; 487 calories

Index

A

aïoli, lime 29
almond and cilantro-crusted chicken with
   lemon mayonnaise 168
angel hair with peas and ricotta 99
arugula
   arugula and pistachio pesto 291
   arugula and red onion salad 131
   arugula salad 231
Asian chicken burgers 147
Asian chicken salad 30

B

bacon mashed potatoes 176
balsamic dressing 366
balsamic vinaigrette 17
barley risotto with chicken and tarragon 164
basil
   basil and oregano steak with
     grilled vegetables 260
   basil pesto 79
   basil tapenade 100
beef
   basil and oregano steak with
     grilled vegetables 260
   beef coconut curry 268
   beef and mushroom stir fry 275
   beef salad with fennel and balsamic
     vinaigrette 17
   beef tenderloin with horseradish herb crust
     and arugula salad 231
   black bean, beef and asparagus stir fry 276
   chili t-bones with hash browns 243
   Chinese ground beef and spicy
     green beans 279
   fajitas and guacamole 263
   filet mignon with caramelized shallots
     and mashed potatoes 244
   filet mignon stuffed with spinach,
     cheese and pepper with parmesan
     mashed potatoes 251
   five-spice ginger beef 272
   hamburger with a twist 232
   honey barbecued steak 235
   kofta with fresh green onion couscous 256
   Mexican spiced steak and chili beans 264
   Moroccan beef with citrus couscous 248
   New York strip steaks with
     lemon thyme butter 236
   potato wedges with sloppy joe topping 252
   Sicilian stuffed pizza 255
   souvlaki with Greek salad 259
   spaghetti and meatballs 104
   steak diane 240

steak salad with blue cheese dressing 21
steak sandwich with tarragon and
   tomato salsa 239
steak teriyaki 271
steaks with blue cheese butter and
   pear salad 228
steaks with mashed parsnips and potatoes 247
Thai beef patties with noodle salad 267
Thai beef salad 22
twice-fried Szechwan beef 280
black bean, beef and asparagus stir fry 276
blue cheese dressing 21
burgers
   Asian chicken 147
   falafel 54
   hamburger with a twist 232
   Italian-style 120
   Thai fish burger 205

C

Caesar dressing 9
Caesar salad, chicken 9
Cajun chicken with chunky salsa 152
cardamom-crusted lamb chops with
   saffron spinach risotto 358
cheese
   angel hair with peas and ricotta 99
   blue cheese dressing 21
   chicken with fontina, pancetta and sage 128
   chicken with ham and cheese 116
   chicken with herb cheese sauce 124
   feta, spinach and prosciutto lamb rolls
     with herbed potatoes 346
   four-cheese sauce 103
   grilled vegetable and ricotta stack 18
   ricotta gnocchi with fresh tomato sauce 107
   ricotta and spinach ravioli with
     pumpkin sauce 83
   spinach, feta and red pepper pizza 13
chermoulla 175
chicken
   almond and cilantro-crusted chicken
     with lemon mayonnaise 168
   Asian chicken burgers 147
   Asian chicken salad 30
   barley risotto with chicken and tarragon 164
   burgers Italian-style 120
   Cajun chicken with chunky salsa 152
   chermoulla chicken with chickpea salad 175
   chicken Caesar salad 9
   chicken chowder 45
   chicken with fontina, pancetta and sage 128
   chicken with ham and cheese 116
   chicken with herb cheese sauce 124
   chicken with honey mustard sauce 167

chicken with horseradish cream
   and sautéed spinach 171
chicken kebabs with herb salad 143
chicken and leek puff pastry squares 53
chicken, lemon and artichoke skewers 132
chicken in lettuce leaf cups 148
chicken, mushroom and fennel pies 136
chicken and mushroom stir fry with
   crispy noodles 159
chicken with parmesan polenta
   and salsa verde 139
chicken and pecan pasta salad 76
chicken alla pizzaiola 172
chicken with pistachio sauce and
   mashed sweet potatoes 135
chicken stuffed with artichokes and
   sun-dried tomatoes 131
chicken tacos with guacamole and
   fresh salsa 50
chicken tandoori wraps with raita 62
cranberry-glazed chicken wraps 127
farfalle with chicken, spinach and tomato 71
fettucine with chicken and mushroom
   cream sauce 67
fried chicken with buttermilk mashed
   potatoes and gravy 123
hoisin chicken stir fry 163
Portuguese-style chicken 144
prosciutto-wrapped chicken legs
   with creamy orzo 119
red curry chicken 155
sesame chicken stir fry 151
spiced chicken with fruity couscous 140
sweet and spicy chicken with noodles 160
Thai chicken noodle soup 58
Thai lime chicken with bok choy 156
chili lime dressing 26, 30
chili t-bones with hash browns 243
chili tomato sauce 365
Chinese barbecued duck salad 26
Chinese ground beef and spicy green beans 279
chowder, chicken 45
citrus couscous 248
coconut rice 201
cod
   cod with grilled corn salad 193
   sweet and sour 210
   Thai fish burger 205
corn, grilled, salad 193
couscous 221
   citrus 248
cranberry-glazed chicken wraps 127
curry
   beef coconut 268
   Madras 345
   red curry chicken 155

D

dijon vinaigrette 308
doner kebab 357
dressing 202 *see also* vinaigrette
    balsamic 366
    blue cheese 21
    Caesar 9
    chili lime 26, 30
    ginger 38
    lemon 295
    lemon oregano 25
    sweet chili 33
    sweet and sour 37
    tomato, caper and walnut 225
duck
    Chinese barbecued duck salad 26
    duck breasts with fig sauce and spinach orzo 179
    duck breasts with five-spice and
        honey peaches 180

E

eggs
    poached, with sage brown butter
        and asparagus 10
    tomato leek frittata with spinach salad 57
endive salad with shrimp, pink grapefruit
    and lime aïoli 29

F

fajitas and guacamole 263
falafel burgers 54
farfalle with chicken, spinach and tomato 71
farfalle, creamy, with fried zucchini 92
fattoush salad 350
fennel-flavored veal chops with
    garlic mustard butter 299
feta, spinach and prosciutto lamb rolls with
    herbed potatoes 346
fettucine
    chicken and mushroom cream sauce, with 67
    grilled vegetables and basil tapenade, with 100
    sausage and tomato cream sauce, with 87
fish *see* seafood
five-spice ginger beef 272
four-cheese sauce 103
frittata, tomato leek, with spinach salad 57

G

ginger dressing 38
gnocchi
    breaded veal cutlets with gnocchi in
        garlic mushroom sauce 283
    ricotta gnocchi with fresh tomato sauce 107
    spinach cream sauce, with 88

Greek pasta salad 25
Greek salad 259, 295
guacamole 263

H

halibut with tomato, caper and walnut
    dressing 225
hamburger with a twist 232
hoisin chicken stir fry 163
honey barbecued steak 235
honey and five-spice lamb with bok choy 338
honey mustard pork chops with celeriac salad 300

I

iskander kebab 365
Italian-style burgers 120

J

jerk-spiced pork loin with butternut squash fries 331

K

kebabs, chicken, with herb salad 143
kofta with fresh green onion couscous 256

L

lamb
    cardamom-crusted lamb chops with
        saffron spinach risotto 358
    doner kebab 357
    feta, spinach and prosciutto lamb rolls
        with herbed potatoes 346
    grilled lamb with fattoush salad 350
    grilled lamb with ratatouille 366
    honey and five-spice lamb with bok choy 338
    iskander kebab 365
    lamb with white wine mascarpone sauce 362
    Mongolian lamb stir fry 353
    paprika dusted lamb loin with tomato
        feta salad 342
    parmesan-breaded lamb chops 368
    rack of lamb with garlic and sage 354
    spicy lamb with fried noodles 361
    spicy lamb with tabbouleh salad 349
    spicy sausage pasta bake 72
    tamarind glazed rack of lamb with Asian
        greens and orange salad 341
    warm pasta provençale salad 80
lemon
    lemon dressing 295
    lemon mayonnaise 168
    lemon oregano dressing 25
    lemon spaetzle 288
    lemon thyme butter 236

lime aïoli 29
linguine with pesto, beans and potatoes 79
linguine with shrimp, peas, lemon and dill 75
lobster tails with lime butter and pineapple
    mint salsa 186

M

Madras curry 345
mango salsa 185
marjoram and lemon-grilled veal chops
    with Greek salad 295
marmalade-glazed pork chops 304
Mexican spiced pork with avocado salsa 315
Mexican spiced steak and chili beans 264
Mongolian lamb stir fry 353
Moroccan beef with citrus couscous 248
Moroccan spiced fish with couscous 221
mustard-crusted rack of veal with mashed
    sweet potatoes 296

N

niçoise salade 41
noodles
    pad Thai 112
    pork and noodle stir fry 323
    seared tuna with wasabi soba noodles 206
    Singapore noodles 115
    spicy lamb with fried noodles 361
    stir-fried pork with bok choy and
        rice noodles 336
    sweet and spicy chicken with noodles 160
    Thai beef patties with noodle salad 267
    Thai chicken noodle soup 58

O

octopus, grilled, salad 34

P

pad Thai 112
pancetta wrapped fish with
    herb-caper butter 190
panzanella salad 14
pappardelle with roasted tomato,
    spinach and feta 108
paprika dusted lamb loin with
    tomato feta salad 342
parmesan-breaded lamb chops 368
pasta
    angel hair with peas and ricotta 99
    chicken and pecan pasta salad 76
    creamy farfalle with fried zucchini 92
    duck breasts with fig sauce and
        spinach orzo 179
    farfalle with chicken, spinach and tomato 71

fettucine with chicken and mushroom
    cream sauce 67
fettucine with grilled vegetables and
    basil tapenade 100
fettucine with sausage and tomato
    cream sauce 87
four-cheese pasta bake 103
gnocchi with spinach cream sauce 88
Greek pasta salad 25
linguine with pesto, beans and potatoes 79
linguine with shrimp, peas, lemon and dill 75
pad Thai 112
pappardelle with roasted tomato,
    spinach and feta 108
penne with grilled vegetables and
    sun-dried tomato mayonnaise 91
penne puttanesca 64
ricotta gnocchi with fresh tomato sauce 107
ricotta and spinach ravioli with pumpkin sauce 83
rigatoni with bacon and asparagus 95
rigatoni bolognese 96
rotini with crisp salami and tomato sauce 111
Singapore noodles 115
spaghetti with garlic and breadcrumbs 84
spaghetti and meatballs 104
spaghetti with mussels and clams 68
spicy sausage pasta bake 72
warm pasta provençale salad 80
pear, roasted, Belgian endive and spinach salad 42
penne with grilled vegetables and sun-dried
    tomato mayonnaise 91
penne puttanesca 64
pesto
    arugula and pistachio 291
    basil 79
    sun-dried tomato 18
pies, chicken, mushroom and fennel 136
pineapple mint salsa 186
piri piri dipping sauce 331
pizza
    pizza sandwich supreme 46
    Sicilian stuffed 255
    spinach, feta and red pepper 13
pork
    barbecued spareribs with red cabbage
        coleslaw 303
    curried fried rice with pork and shrimp 320
    honey mustard pork chops with celeriac salad 300
    jerk-spiced pork loin with butternut
        squash fries 331
    Madras curry 345
    marmalade-glazed pork chops 304
    Mexican spiced pork with avocado salsa 315
    pork chops with goat cheese and
        beet salad 308
    pork larb with broccolini 335

pork and lemongrass stir fry 332
pork, lime and peanut salad 33
pork and noodle stir fry 323
pork and peapods 319
pork with sweet and sour peaches 327
pork tacos with corn salsa 312
pork tenderloin with orange and fennel 311
quick pork fried rice 324
rigatoni bolognese 96
roast pork with mustard and caramelized
    apples 307
sticky pork with veggies 316
stir-fried pork with bok choy and
    rice noodles 336
teriyaki pork with pineapple 328
Portuguese-style chicken 144
potatoes
    bacon mashed potatoes 176
    potato wedges with sloppy joe topping 252
poultry see chicken; duck; turkey
prosciutto-wrapped chicken legs with
    creamy orzo 119
puff pastry squares, chicken and leek 53

R

raita 62
red cabbage coleslaw 303
red curry chicken 155
red pepper remoulade 197
rice see also risotto
    coconut 201
    curried fried rice with pork and shrimp 320
    quick pork fried rice 324
ricotta gnocchi with fresh tomato sauce 107
ricotta and spinach ravioli with pumpkin sauce 83
rigatoni with bacon and asparagus 95
rigatoni bolognese 96
risotto see also rice
    barley risotto with chicken and tarragon 164
    cardamom-crusted lamb chops with
        saffron spinach risotto 358
    quick-and-easy shrimp and pea risotto 194
    risotto Milanese 284
rotini with crisp salami and tomato sauce 111

S

salade niçoise 41
salads
    arugula 231
    arugula and red onion 131
    Asian chicken 30
    beef salad with fennel and balsamic
        vinaigrette 17
    chicken Caesar 9
    chicken and pecan pasta 76
    Chinese barbecued duck 26

endive salad with shrimp, pink grapefruit
    and lime aïoli 29
fattoush 350
Greek 259, 295
Greek pasta 25
grilled corn 193
grilled octopus 34
pan-fried tofu with cabbage 37
panzanella 14
pork, lime and peanut 33
red cabbage coleslaw 303
roasted pear, Belgian endive and spinach 42
salade niçoise 41
shrimp and avocado salad with
    ginger dressing 38
smoked salmon and avocado 61
steak salad with blue cheese dressing 21
steaks with blue cheese butter
    and pear salad 228
tabbouleh 349
tempura shrimp 217
Thai beef 22
warm pasta provençale 80
white bean 287
salmon
    salmon with garlic ginger butter 226
    salmon phyllo triangles 222
    salmon in sesame crust 182
    salmon with spinach, fennel and
        apple salad 218
    salt and Szechwan pepper salmon
        with wasabi mayonnaise 189
salsa
    avocado 6
    chunky 152
    corn 312
    fresh 50
    mango 185
    pineapple mint 186
    tarragon and tomato 239
    verde 139
salt and Szechwan pepper salmon with
    wasabi mayonnaise 189
saltimbocca with risotto Milanese 284
sandwiches/wraps
    chicken tandoori wraps with raita 62
    cranberry-glazed chicken wraps 127
    pizza sandwich supreme 46
    steak sandwich with tarragon and
        tomato salsa 239
sauces
    chili tomato 365
    four-cheese 103
    piri piri dipping sauce 331
    yogurt and tahini 54
scallops, grilled, with papaya salsa 49

seafood
    cod with grilled corn salad 193
    endive salad with shrimp, pink grapefruit
       and lime aïoli 29
    grilled octopus salad 34
    grilled scallops with papaya salsa 49
    grilled shrimp with tropical fruits 202
    halibut with tomato, caper and
       walnut dressing 225
    linguine with shrimp, peas, lemon and dill 75
    lobster tails with lime butter and
       pineapple mint salsa 186
    Moroccan spiced fish with couscous 221
    pancetta wrapped fish with
       herb-caper butter 190
    pan-fried fish with roasted ratatouille 213
    quick-and-easy shrimp and pea risotto 194
    salmon with garlic ginger butter 226
    salmon phyllo triangles 222
    salmon in sesame crust 182
    salmon with spinach, fennel and
       apple salad 218
    salt and Szechwan pepper salmon
       with wasabi mayonnaise 189
    seared tuna with wasabi soba noodles 206
    shrimp, asparagus and sesame stir fry 209
    shrimp and avocado salad with
       ginger dressing 38
    shrimp fritters with avocado salsa 6
    shrimp and swordfish skewers
       with coconut rice 201
    smoked salmon and avocado salad 61
    snapper with red pepper remoulade
       and fried potatoes 197
    spaghetti with mussels and clams 68
    spicy grilled shrimp with fresh mango salsa 185
    sweet and sour cod 210
    swordfish skewers with mashed
       potatoes and skordalia 214
    tempura shrimp salad 217
    Thai fish burger 205
    tilapia with chunky tomato caper sauce 198
sesame chicken stir fry 151
shrimp
    curried fried rice with pork and shrimp 320
    endive salad with shrimp, pink grapefruit
       and lime aïoli 29
    grilled shrimp with tropical fruits 202
    linguine with shrimp, peas, lemon and dill 75
    quick-and-easy shrimp and pea risotto 194
    shrimp, asparagus and sesame stir fry 209
    shrimp and avocado salad with
       ginger dressing 38
    shrimp fritters with avocado salsa 6
    shrimp and swordfish skewers
       with coconut rice 201

spicy grilled shrimp with fresh mango salsa 185
tempura shrimp salad 217
Sicilian stuffed pizza 255
Singapore noodles 115
skordalia 214
smoked salmon and avocado salad 61
snapper with red pepper remoulade
    and fried potatoes 197
soups
    Thai chicken noodle 58
souvlaki with Greek salad 259
spaghetti
    meatballs, and 104
    mussels and clams, with 68
    spaghetti with garlic and breadcrumbs 84
    spaghetti and meatballs 104
spareribs, barbecued, with red cabbage
    coleslaw 303
spiced chicken with fruity couscous 140
spicy lamb with fried noodles 361
spicy lamb with tabbouleh salad 349
spicy sausage pasta bake 72
spinach, feta and red pepper pizza 13
sticky pork with veggies 316
stir fries
    beef and mushroom 275
    black bean, beef and asparagus 276
    chicken and mushroom stir fry
      with crispy noodles 159
    hoisin chicken 163
    Mongolian lamb 353
    pork and lemongrass 332
    pork and noodle 323
    sesame chicken 151
    shrimp, asparagus and sesame 209
    stir-fried pork with bok choy and rice noodles 336
sweet chili dressing 33
sweet and sour cod 210
sweet and sour dressing 37
sweet and spicy chicken with noodles 160
swordfish skewers with mashed potatoes
    and skordalia 214
Szechwan beef, twice-fried 280

T

tabbouleh salad 349
tacos
    chicken tacos with guacamole and
      fresh salsa 50
    pork, with corn salsa 312
tamarind glazed rack of lamb with Asian greens
    and orange salad 341
tapenade, basil 100
tarragon and tomato salsa 239
tempura shrimp salad 217

teriyaki pork with pineapple 328
teriyaki, steak 271
Thai beef patties with noodle salad 267
Thai beef salad 22
Thai chicken noodle soup 58
Thai fish burger 205
Thai lime chicken with bok choy 156
tilapia with chunky tomato caper sauce 198
tofu, pan-fried, with cabbage salad 37
tomato
    sun-dried tomato pesto 18
    tomato, caper and walnut dressing 225
    tomato leek frittata with spinach salad 57
    vinaigrette 14
tuna, seared, with wasabi soba noodles 206
turkey
    turkey cutlets with mustard cream sauce
      and bacon mashed potatoes 176

V

veal
    breaded veal cutlets with gnocchi in
      garlic mushroom sauce 283
    fennel-flavored veal chops with
      garlic mustard butter 299
    marjoram and lemon-grilled veal chops
      with Greek salad 295
    mustard-crusted rack of veal with
      mashed sweet potatoes 296
    rigatoni bolognese 96
    saltimbocca with risotto Milanese 284
    veal cutlets with white bean salad 287
    veal with mushrooms and mustard
      cream sauce 292
    veal scallopine with arugula and
      pistachio pesto 291
    wiener schnitzel with lemon spaetzle 288
vegetable, grilled, and ricotta stack 18
vinaigrette 41 see also dressings
    balsamic 17
    dijon 308
    tomato 14

W

white bean salad 287
wiener schnitzel with lemon spaetzle 288

Y

yogurt and tahini sauce 54